DREAMING HISTORY

DREAMING HISTORY

*A Collection of Wisconsin
Native-American Writing*

Edited by Mary Anne Doan
& Jim Stevens

PRAIRIE OAK PRESS
Madison, Wisconsin

First edition, first printing
Copyright ©1995 by Jim Stevens and Mary Anne Doan

Prairie Oak Press
821 Prospect Place
Madison, Wisconsin 53703

Cover illustration by Dawn Dark Mountain
Typeset by KC Graphics, Inc., Madison, Wisconsin
Printed in the United States of America by BookCrafters,
    Chelsea, Michigan

Library of Congress Cataloging-in-Publication Data

Dreaming history: a collection of Wisconsin Native-American writing /
    edited by Mary Anne Doan and Jim Stevens. -- 1st ed.
        p.   cm.
    ISBN 1-879483-26-2 : $10.95
    1. American literature--Indian authors. 2. Indians of North
America--Wisconsin--Literary collections. 3. American literature--
Wisconsin. I. Doan, Mary Anne. II. Stevens, Jim, 1939–   .
PS508.I5D74 1995   95-1752
810.8'08970775--dc20   CIP

In Memory of Menominee poet Gerti Sennett
Kah-shee-nau-wah (Morning of the Red Dawn)
1919-1994

Seeded into the warm womb of the old woman,
I fed upon her motherbreast
And felt the spirit of me growing
With the strength and wisdom of her . . .

from *Dream Song to the Buffalo Spirit,*
1990, Wisconsin Arts Press

INTRODUCTION

. . . deep maps of the land . . .

Early on the Saturday morning of August 20, 1994 near Janesville, Wisconsin, Dave Heider was walking hopefully on the wooded hill of his buffalo pasture. He was thinking that one of the females of his small herd was giving birth, for she was not with the others. During this special time, he knew, the mothers usually went off by themselves.

And then at the far southeast corner of the yard, he saw the two. The calf was already free of her mother's water, born perhaps two-and-a-half hours earlier. And she was pure white, coming out when Moon was approaching full.

Heider knew this was a rare animal. But in his first thoughts, he had no awareness of the calf's significance within Native-American legends. Within days, of necessity, he came in communication with Lakota elders, who told him of the small one's relationship with White Buffalo Calf Woman, a great teacher among them over a thousand years.

Since around 900, it is specially remembered, she has been returning to Mother Earth bearing spiritual gifts. And within the prayers carried by Lakota People, the first of these responsibilities is the Great Pipe, the Sacred Pipe for sending prayers to the Creator. We speak particularly here of responsibility, for the Pipe is of Earth and her creatures, is of nativity and the peoples living within.

We are thinking that this recent event should have been no surprise. The original receptivity was available to European-Americans from the beginning on Turtle Island (North

America), had there been a slowing to hear, a willingness to listen.

We are remembering, for example, that people from Europe were once called Younger Brother in formal council with Native-Americans. We are remembering the true place of the Irokwa in the development of the government of the United States. And we are remembering the real sharing and giving of things, the many foods, the means of planting, which took place in those early days in a pristine land which was so new and frightening for the peoples from Europe.

We are remembering a new people becoming more and more uncentered in materiality as they learned to see with the eye rather than with the heart, with the spirit.

As we are coming to these thoughts of the White Buffalo Calf, at the same time we are recalling the words of Oren Lyons, one of the Faithkeepers of the Onandaga and the Six Nations who are Irokwa, who speaks with deliberation and reverence of the Good Mind, universal mind, which shall dream moments such as the White Buffalo Calf into existence. He is speaking of Great Law, the natural law, which has no place for exalting egotism, so wastefully prevalent on Earth today.

"We have a long perspective," he has said. "We've been in one place a long time. We've seen the Sun come up in the same place many hundreds, thousands of years. And so we have a familiarity with the earth itself. The elements, we know about them. . . . The ceremonies carry forward this respect. . . . And so we have these wellsprings of knowledge, the long term thinking required for proper context."

We are happy that this collection, *Dreaming History*, by Wisconsin Native-American writers, has been published in this special time of return, for it makes our path all the more clear. During the week as this is being written, approaching November election day of the dominant culture, we are aware of the sales pitches being presented within the American media, which stress overriding fear of almost everything within the world. The televisions are bloated with it.

And while it is certain that we are all in this together, that Native-American people also are facing the abyss, as we have for five-hundred years, (see Kimberly Blaeser's "On the Way to the Chicago Pow-wow"), a great difference in approach has to do with the way one *knows* of it. Cooperation, reciprocity between all living things, balance, are utterly critical in this special, difficult time.

Native-American peoples have a special perspective, which is part of being so connected to the energies of Mother Earth. The world crucially needs this indigenous perspective if we are all to survive. It is our responsibility to Mother Earth to share the old knowledge. It is a knowledge which all peoples of the Earth at one time held in common.

This is not arrogance, it is sharing. Those who live within the diverse original cultures of Turtle Island tend to face our many uncertainties with clarity, as seeing mystery. This thinking is for the seven generations to come. We see things continually renewing themselves from the womb of life. It is a wholesome approach which pervades the poetry and prose of this book.

The pieces collected within these pages have as their wellspring the songs, stories and oratory which have been part of the Native civilizations for thousands of years. Contemporary indigenous writers, many of them graduates of university writing and literature programs, have learned well the ways of the dominant culture, while still holding to the magic of the people gone before. We have learned to remain within the oral, communal, power thru our writings.

We hope that thru this spirit you will enter into these words, for within these pages you will find the thoughts coming very much from an earth house, in a true sense one of the original houses. That you may enter into these passages, seeing with these writers the extraordinary in the ordinary, we pray you shall open your hearts also, helping you to see the Great Web of Life once again.

We have found it proper to arrange the poetry and prose of *Dreaming History* in four sections. These correspond to the four directions, the great world quarters of the sacred circle. In each section, then, we are addressing the spiritual qualities of the particular direction. As you proceed thru this collection, in a real sense, you shall be walking around the Path of Life.

The first part, "Listening to the Voices," is of the East, of Springtime. Here is the direction where Sun comes up, where Mother Earth is born, where light and clarity comes into our orb and wonder comes into our life.

Part Two, "Living the World," is of the South, Summertime. Here the pieces address the understanding of living in harmony and of learning to be who you are. South is the place of being within a larger community.

The West and Autumn are within the third section, "Teaching and Prayers." The West is the direction of receiving and darkness. Here is where all ideas are born. It is the place of the womb and looking within, the place of knowing the future through correspondence with the Spirits.

Part Four, "Talking Indian," is of North and Winter, the place and time of the retelling of the legends of the community, the direction of knowing thru the experience which has gone before. Here is where the summing up occurs, the "winter count," coming before the birthtime of Spring.

These are the experiences recounted within *Dreaming History*. The writers represented in these pages are all living in Wisconsin, all part of a land which is in a real sense still Indian Country. We are as hawks in this land, part of the Great Tree among the Sacred Hills, gathering the embers of our lives.

Mary Anne Doan
Jim Stevens

November 8, 1994

ACKNOWLEDGMENTS

We wish to thank the many people who have given of their help in organizing and preparing this collection. Among them are Kimberly Blaeser, Charlene Blue Horse, Rod Clark, Andy Connors, Bree Doan, Anne Kingsbury, Ken Metoxen, Robert Miller, Mike Roberts, Rose Mary Robinson, Jan Saiz, Francis Steindorf, Randy Tallmadge, Roxanne Tallmadge and Roberta Whiteman.

Special gratitude is due Jerry Minnich and Kristin Visser of Prairie Oak Press, who originally proposed this collection, as well as all the elders and healers of the Native-American community, from whom we are well learning.

Grateful thanks are also due Wisconsin Oneida Arts Program and Potawatomi Bingo and Casino for their support of this project. Nyahweh. Miigwetch.

CONTENTS

INTRODUCTION...vii

ACKNOWLEDGMENTS...............................xi

1   LISTENING TO THE VOICES........................1

The Search (Mary Anne Doan) 3
journey of the circle (Rose Mary Robinson) 6
Where I Was That Day (Kimberly Blaeser) 8
My Wind Chimes (Gladyce Nahbenayash)................11
Flying On One Wing (Ellen Kort)........................12
The Place of Meeting (Jim Stevens) 14
"The Day Comes When You See Each Other"
    (Kenneth Brickman Metoxen) 16

2   LIVING THE WORLD 19

What The Circle Means (Michael Roberts) 21
Sea Turtle (Ellen Kort) 23
The Pow-Wow Trail BEGINS
    (Kenneth Brickman Metoxen) 25
The Planted Ones (Ellen Kort) 26
Energy Exchanged (Gladyce Nahbenayash).............28
Twenty Five or Fifty Cents (Charlene Blue Horse)........29
The Fall (Charlene Blue Horse)..........................36
Woman (Rose Mary Robinson)..........................37
Flute-Player (Ellen Kort)................................38
Song to Carry the Virgin Places (Jim Stevens) 40
Medicine Woman (Ellen Kort)...........................42
After the Sweat (Charlene Blue Horse) 43
Fragments: Dance and Vision (Michael Roberts) 45
Aunt Marie's Visit (Gladyce Nahbenayash)..............47

Patience (Pamela Green LaBarge) 50
Tractor (Charlene Blue Horse). 51

3   TEACHING AND PRAYERS 57

Language of the Birds (Gladyce Nahbenayash) 59
Like the Snowflake (Andrew Connors) 60
The Moon Bear (Pamela Green LaBarge). 64
Vision Seeker (Ellen Kort). 66
Keys (Gladyce Nahbenayash). 67
Those Things That Come To You At Night
    (Kimberly Blaeser). 69
Cochiti Buffalo Dance (Kenneth Brickman Metoxen) 72
Let Me Be A Light (Mary Ann Doan) 74
Overland Skiing (Gladyce Nahbenayash). 76
I Dance Around the Turtle's Back (Jim Stevens) 78
Two Sections from a Short Longhouse
    Thanksgiving Offering (Michael Roberts) 80
Wagluh' TaTapi (Charlene Blue Horse) 82
The Giveaway (Mary Anne Doan). 85
Camping With Our Relatives (Gladyce Nahbenayash).... 87
aniishinaabe song (Rose Mary Robinson) 88
"Truckers say they" (Kenneth Brickman Metoxen) 89

4   TALKING INDIAN. 91

Meeting Place (Kimberly Blaeser) 93
The Plumed Snail (Jim Stevens) 95
Indian Talk (Charlene Blue Horse) 99
Maybe I Should've Worn a Feather (Michael Roberts) ... 101
Living History (Kimberly Blaeser). 103
Poem For Our Ancestors (Charlene Blue Horse) 104
When (Rose Mary Robinson) 106
On the Way to the Chicago Pow-Wow
    (Kimberly Blaeser). 107
Feeling Watched (Charlene Blue Horse) 109
Niimi's Song: Traveling Thunder (Andrew Connors) 111
"Whitefish Bay" (Kenneth Brickman Metoxen). 113

FURTHER READING AND VIEWING 115

NOTES ON THE WRITERS. 119

Part I

LISTENING TO THE VOICES

In this first section, we have gathered works which express the first steps taken on the Native-American path, the first days when the community of Spirits came into our lives, those first moments of seeing. This first section is about truly listening.

For some of us, these first steps as Native-Americans came later in our lives. Others of us were blessed with being raised within traditional means. But for all of us, being Native-American has meant a continual native-regaining process in the midst of a dominant culture, in which every step we take from the balls of our feet has to be an utterly conscious one. We remind ourselves that we dream as Grandfather Sun raises into Sky.

Within "The Search," Mary Anne Doan is writing lyrically of the process of self-discovery and of knowing at last that her origins were to be found through the Spirit of her grandmother.

In "journey of the circle," Rose Mary Robinson is expressing the spiritual journey which has been her life, and of being always guided on the path by the inner voice which is knowing in the ways of the world.

Kimberly Blaeser, in "Where I Was That Day," tells of the first time she found herself truly seeing the worlds of the Spirit.

1

In "My Wind Chimes," Gladyce Nahbenayash sings of the beautiful dance of the spirit which comes through natural energy.

Ellen Kort, in "Flying On One Wing," recognizes the terrors accompanying the passage through the rim of darkness.

Jim Stevens, in "The Place of Meeting," writes of the sounds and sights attending a first meeting with his cousins of the Irokwa Nation.

And in the closing poem of this first section, Ken Metoxen presents us with a native benediction, as he sings of the insight leading a person to the very powerful thoughts of the relations all of us carry.

Mary Anne Doan

The Search

Where are you my Grandmother?
I have searched for you
For all my years
Among the red rocks of Sedona
The Anasazi caves of Bandelara
The forests of Canada
The Redwoods
The Sierra Madres
And still I know not
Where you began,
Where you are,
And where
The two of us, shall meet.

I have asked
to see you in my dreams,
But still you do not come . . .
And yet,
an Indian maid,

A spirit guide,
Has always come
to me
in prayer.
She calls herself
Inea,
Could you
Be she?

There is a constant pulling
At my heart
that draws me
ever deeper
to the things I sense
Were such a part of you.
Embedded here,
Within my yearning breast,
Imprisoned.
Waiting for me
to find the answers
and set your spirit free at last.

I wonder if, my Grandmother
I do not find you
Because you
Are also lost?
Lost to the ways of your people,
Lost far from your ancestral home,
Lost long ago
Without a Dream
To guide you.
Lost in an alien world
In which, I too, am such a part.

There is so much
I would like to ask you,
My Grandmother,
So much, that
I thirst to understand.

Why do I dream of wolves
And eagles swirling above my head
As if they knew a secret
I was meant to find?
And why, at centuries of pain
caused my brothers red
and my heart is crushed in grief
I can not stop the flow of tears
so strong, I feel in each new death
a part of me, has also died . . .
And how is it,
The gentle deer
Walks straight to me
Nudging my shoulder
with wet nose
not a fear,
as if greeting
a long lost sister
a tender hello?
And why do all plants growing green
Shout out to me
to learn their healing medicines
to find my power here within
and use it where the need is great?
And why oh Grandmother
Must I flee
Far from cities pounding roar
to woods and streams and mountains high,
To share communion
with the Earth
And feel the peace She brings?

Where are you, my Grandmother?

Anasazi, Sedona, Bandelara: Anasazi is a Dine (Navaho) word meaning "The ancient ones" of the Southwest. Sedona is a wilderness spiritual area, lately becoming increasingly invaded by tourists. Bandelara was one of the cliff pueblos of the Anasazi.

Rose Mary Robinson

journey of the circle

and so i go on journeys far and wide,
and walk the distant hills
and watch the ever-closer stars
and hear the wind around my hair.

i follow, trembling as i climb
the rocks, no path laid out
that i can see, and yet
as i look backward, there behind
a trail is carved
for others who would follow me.

where do i go and who the voice
that beckons me? sometimes i wonder
at the yearning deep inside
but mostly do i climb, unknowing
yet not blind.

and sometimes do i almost understand
the medicines that grow with me
and comfort give when i am lost
but not alone.

and sometimes as i see a glimpse
of life beyond the sky, i run
renewed with courage and the strength
of eagle wings.

there is no sense of ending
as i listen longingly, awake
to songs within my drum.
who sings to me? and who am i
to know the music of the one
who calls to me?

Kimberly Blaeser

Where I Was That Day

It wasn't just the pill bugs
gray, many-legged and pulling that stunt
like they always did
closing in on themselves
contracting into the tiny round mass
like an image of the origin circle
And it wasn't the turtle alone either
who became so neatly one half of the earth's sphere

It was partly that day when I stopped at the little creek
and noticed the funny bumps on that floating log
and how they seemed to be looking at me
and how they were really little heads with beady bulging eyes
and how when I came back a half an hour later
the bumps had been rearranged on that log

It was partly the butterflies that would materialize
out of the flower blossoms
and the deer that appeared and disappeared into the forest
while standing stalk still

whose shape would be invisible one minute
and would stand out clearly the next
like the image in one of the connect-the-dot puzzles

It was the stick bugs, the chameleon
the snakes that became branches
the opossum who was dead then suddenly alive
And it was me who fit and saw one minute so clearly
and then stumbled blind the next
that made me think we are all always finding our place
in the great sphere of creation
that made me know I could learn a way
to pull the world around me too
to color myself with earth and air and water
and so become indistinguishable
to match my breath to the one
to pulse in and out with the mystery
to be both still and wildly alive in the same moment
to be strangely absent from myself
and yet feel large as all creation
to know
to know
to know and to belong
while the spell holds
learning to hold it a little longer each time

That's where I was that day
I watched you from the arbor
never blinking
while you looked all about for me
and then turned back home
thinking to find me in another place
when I was there everywhere you looked
I knew then the stories about Geronimo were true
and that he did turn to stone
while the cavalries passed him by
mistook him for just a part of the mountain
when he had really become the whole mountain

and all the air they breathed
and even the dust beneath their horse's hooves

I walk about trying to find the place I was that day
but getting there seems harder now
I feel heavier, my spirit weighted down
and I'm thinking I must shed something
like the animals shed their hair or skin
lose even their antlers annually
while I hold on to everything
and I'm thinking I must change my colors
like the rabbit, the ptarmigan, the weasel
and I'm thinking I must hibernate and fast
feed off my own excess for a season
and then perhaps emerge
in the place I was that day
and stay there longer this time

And I walk about and watch the creatures
the tree toads becoming and unbecoming a part of the trunk
the rocks in my path that crack open into grasshoppers
    and fly away
the spider who hangs suspended before me
and then disappears into thin air
and I feel comforted
knowing we are all
in this puzzle together
knowing we are all just learning
to hold the spell
a little longer
each time

Turtle: Among the many cultures native to our hemisphere, there are origin
legends which refer to a woman falling from a previous world in the sky
and landing on the back of a great turtle. Thus North America is commonly
called Turtle Island by indigenous peoples.

Gladyce Nahbenayash

My Wind Chimes

My wind chimes
Moved by the breeze
Flowing and following the wind spirits naturally
Singing a beautiful wind song
Dancing a wind spirit dance

My self
Also moved by the natural powers
Can not feel or follow the flow
I am resisting and blocked
Can not hear the winds or any element
Being plugged, blocked and frozen
Leads one to a deep sadness
Going against myself and the spirits
Is deadening

Wishing my self transformed
To a wind chime
So I could sing my song
So I could dance my dance

So I could be

Ellen Kort

Flying on One Wing

Skin stretches
thin barely
covers flesh
pulls taut
to this
place where
I throw
my voice
against wind
claw at stars
that leave
scratch marks
across my iris
that have opened
wide into
the black
lens of memory
And this is where
it always begins
where I dredge

for river
for voices
that are my own
voices that howl
and keen
in coming daylight
letting go
of the blessed dark

Jim Stevens

The Place of Meeting

(For Priscilla Manders, Vernon Moon, Janet Malcolm,
Oneida Nation Museum)

For the first time carrying this dream I walk the path up
    from Duck Creek
Day for the giving of leaves, across a winding forest into
    the village where pine trees hold sway

I am coming thru the entrance, Wingeds drum and make
    high circle
And People sing, who remain in their knowledge of the sky

My eyes are going beyond three birches, spreading from
    their feet like Sisters
Across a path made around by the Great Little People

I am entering the Longhouse where the smoke is held in
    honor of all these lives
The fires and voices thru a long room of cornhusk dreaming

So great a peace as it is in the village where I become
    welcomed
Here it is below the hill, lanterns of sumac to turn into
    the Sun
So LifeGiver told this: the way elm bark would hold these
    breaths together
All creatures within a universe where a hand of vines is
    weaving their Thunderer leaves

It is an hour now of thought-forms coming thru me, so a
    blue dragonfly flits across my vision
How was it once spoken on the Island of the Turtle?
People live again with People for the Truth is always in this
    tongue
In a place where blood forever awakens, and my heart is
    deep with the song

Wingeds: birds

Great little people: Among the Six Nations who are the Irokwa, these are
the Jogeho (the e pronounced as in "get"), the fairies who are great helpers
of the people.

Thunderer: The spirit of thunder. Here, the leaves were shaped as in a
common representation of Thunderbird, with the outstretched wings.

15

Kenneth Brickman Metoxen

The day comes you see each other
        a glance, a batter of an eye
He or she there
        Old or young
      poor or rich
                        Black or Native
White or Mixed
                  tall, thin, ugly, beautiful,
    sensuous, vulgar, happy, or lonely

        The mirror is clear as the
    window on your eyelids

        Look, stare, study, believe
                trust, and follow
that intuition of insight

        Because, to ignore that twin's
destiny, or yours, is
                truly to deny fate
    of a fuller you

    Go say hello and have a meal
        on each other

Share your wealth to learn

Twin: Among the indigenous peoples of Turtle Island, there are many detailed, somewhat diverse, stories of these brothers. Among the Oneida, who are one of the Sister Nations of the Irokwa, one brother carries Sky (Above) power, the other Earth (Below) power. The two meet and fight for dominance upon Earth. Sky Brother wins, but the other continues to live beneath the Earth's surface. Thus the legend represents the struggle between what is termed in Western culture good and evil. Among Irokwa, the two brothers simply represent different sides of The One Soul.

Part II

LIVING THE WORLD

The poems and stories of this section are of community and of living in harmoniousness within that experience of the heart. These are pieces expressing faith, and within that place, serious playfulness. But there is also something of Trickster here, something of the shocks to the bodily system which can come from the outside world, but which ultimately can bring one closer inside the love of community.

Michael Roberts' "What The Circle Means" expresses Native-American thoughts about the circularity of the world and of the balance of life within that world. He speaks from Irokwa teachings, but what he expresses finds understanding among all Native-Americans.

In "Sea Turtle," Ellen Kort is recalling her meeting with the spiritually eldest of four-legged creatures, in which she experiences a beautiful communion of the spirit.

Ken Metoxen's "The Pow-Wow Trail BEGINS" recounts something of what occurs as he lives within the powwow community.

Kort's poem, "The Planted Ones," tells of learning from her grandmother.

In "Energy Exchanged," Gladyce Nahbenayash recounts the experience of being with one of her elders, and of the life lessons she learned.

Charlene Blue Horse, in "Twenty Five or Fifty Cents," is telling two stories. The first is of the life within an Indian household. The interior story is of the disharmonious passing of a Lakota Elder. The two stories together are about the power of community.

In "The Fall," Blue Horse presents us with a poem about comforting a grandson.

Rose Mary Robinson's "Woman," expresses the strength of being which is within every Native-American woman.

Ellen Kort's poem "Flute-Player" is about feeling spiritual qualities of Native-American flute.

In "Song to Carry the Virgin Places," Jim Stevens writes of hearing the Cree singer Buffy Sainte-Marie, of the feminine spirituality which emenated from her performance and of the communal power which came to pass.

Kort's "Medicine Woman" is a poem of homage to a healer.

Blue Horse's "After the Sweat" is a poem of being reborn after the traditional ceremony which is a center of healing and community for all Native-Americans.

Roberts' "Fragments: Dance and Vision" is of the spirituality of the dance.

In "Aunt Marie's Visit," Gladyce Nahbenayash speaks of discovering for herself just how close are the material and immaterial worlds and of how important this knowledge is within the Native-American community.

Pamela LaBarge's "Patience" is about receiving lessons from the spirits of her homeplace.

Charlene Blue Horse's "Tractor" is a story about the dangerousness of being with evil spirits, but it is also about the imbalance between the inward and outward communities.

Michael Roberts

What The Circle Means

We see, looking at the horizon and the stars,
how the land we are standing on curves
away in a pattern we can follow,
the sun coming and going at certain times,

the stars being seen again and again
in certain parts of the sky and in certain seasons.
The People always watched these comings and goings
and followed these patterns and saw these curvings

returning again and again. It is so clear over time.
The Sun comes big and yellow from the east, early in
the time of planting, and earliest with all
the warm red winds out of the southern lands.

Then the Three Sisters, the People's plantings, grow dark
and lush swallowing sunlight and days gone short
and black in the west, where the Sun goes always sooner
following the circle we all know after a few years.

The falling white sheet comes out of the north, each season
in this circle, always in this circle, as the Earth
circles the Sun and the Moon the Earth, circling
like the stars and the seasons and the dancers

who are our sisters and cousins.
In the center of our circle is the Earth, who is our mother.
She is riding on the broad back of a turtle, who is hard
and soft in places and walks on the land

and swims through the waters. This turtle is very old
and he has carried us for a long time. Our Mother,
the Earth, fell pregnant with all of us
from another place up in the circling stars,

clutching in her hands dark soil and ripe seeds.
She fell onto this Great Turtle who spread his back wide
and asked his brothers in this world, then all water
without end, to help him save our Mother.

These brothers, the Muskie, the Otter, and the Beaver
dove down into the bottom of the swirling water
and each brought up a little shovel of mud
to make a solid place on Turtle's back.

Where she fell on Turtle became this island
and the seeds and soil in her hands, she spread
all around on Turtle's spreading back.
Our Mother, the Earth, had her children here

and here we are, all of us and we owe so much
to the Muskie and the Otter and the Beaver
and let's not forget we're walking on Turtle
and somehow the stars are our cousins, too.

Three Sisters: Corn, beans and squash, which were traditionally planted
together in a small mound. Thus the three supported each other in growth.

Ellen Kort

Sea Turtle

Tonight she lumbers up from the sea as though she knows I am waiting. Up through snarls of seaweed and plankton. Her front flippers pull hard against wet sand, like an old woman gone heavy. Water spreads out around her into white sea hair, braided silver by the moon. She claws her way up the beach, stopping now and then to bury her nose, the way a dog sniffs at first snow. She goes into the grains of sand, feels how they rub and grind against one another in the night. I can see the big green darkness of her, the humped shell that looks like the earth-spattered, rusted dipper that hung for years on a nail outside my grandfather's barn. Her front flippers are flying now, beating some ancient rhythm that sends showers of sand over her, whirls it into streaks and sparks, voicing it wordless from belly to mouth to sky. Head bowed, slow breathing, gusts fuse sand and sea and moon. She is completely covered. Except for her eyes, which are cleansed by a continuous flow of tears. There is singing. A humming sound. At first I think it's wind strumming the casaurinas, until I feel it rumble inside me. A memory song, bone deep, as familiar as my grandmother's melody for sick children and babies. I hear it

. . . this calling song from my dreams. Is it what brought me here tonight along this lonely stretch of beach? And does the turtle hear it, too? Maybe it's true that we all scatter trails of words and music that are embedded in our footprints. That dream-tracks cover the land, are woven through waves like a map to find our way home. And maybe there's nothing: no tiny grain of sand, no rock, leaf or the smallest trickle of water that can't be sung. Maybe it's the same music the swan makes before she dies, how she finds her true voice just that once. No barking to call her young. No blaring like a bugle or the snort and hiss of anger or fear. Just the plaintive, melodious song as it falls from the sky. All those notes stitched from air, riding the wind. The moon passes through a cloud and the turtle and I are in the black hole she is digging. I am patting the sides while she goes deeper. Sinking front flippers into the sand at the edge of the pit, she lowers the back of her body to the bottom of the hole in the same way my daughter gripped the bed when the baby came ripping through her. The turtle eggs are round and white and she brushes sand over them little by little with her hind flipper until they are covered. I help her fill in the rest. To disguise the location, we churn the sand all around the nest, moving further and further out. I look at the sharp jaw, hooked nose and it is my face, but older. She is tired. I brush sand from the dark map of her shell, wishing I had some of Marianne's wild geranium tea. We sit side by side listening to deep water echo in the distance. I can hear my heart talking inside my head, words that work slowly, pulling the warm starquilt of night close in around us. Words that will store this image on the back wall of my mind. She moves then. Slowly, into the widening waves. I breathe time as she breathes water . . . water we are buried in and rise from . . . until there is only her dark shadow after-image. I try to get beyond aloneness into the greening light that brushes over the beach. It's as though I'm sitting somewhere else, watching the night play itself out against a watercolor of sky and water. I bed down between the tough knuckles of driftwood. It is almost morning.

Kenneth Brickman Metoxen

The Pow-wow Trail BEGINS

July 4th '91
Oneida Pow-wow:
 Ken Powless, 79 from Oklahoma, was teaching me ways to dance traditional. He is Oneida. When my father went to Haskell, Ken treated him well.
 Ken told me about the hunt and warrior dances. That, when I make a movement to make it with a purpose and mean it. We danced the whole Pow-wow together. He won in the elder contest.

Friday July 12, '91
White Fish Bay Pow-wow
 I went with Gene Delcourt in a campus van to do his report on Pow-wow Rebirth. We talked about the military, women, wives, children, laughter, songs, friends, etc. etc. etc.
 I saw beautiful dancers, male, female, and unforgetable drums, and Oneida friends. Stan Webster was there. I cut the tail off of a beaver but that nite I left it out. Something took it. I feel sorry for the beaver. It was on the side of the road dead. To pass on without a body part not used. I felt guilt. I pray an animal ate it all. I pray a lot for forgiveness and to honor the animals, all of them.

Ellen Kort

The Planted Ones

Grandmother stored beans
in glass jars on the pantry shelf
named favorites   Wind Runner
Yellow Eye   Hawk Tail

Late in spring she poked
her fingers into warm ground
making nests   for the last
vegetable to be planted

She loved brushstrokes of green
Blossoms   Beans at work building
houses   Little swollen moons
wrapping their spines up and over

weaving   catching the day's sun
morning's wet mouth   She knew
them as surely as her ancestors
knew which ones held their seeds

the careless ones who broke free
too early   She counted days
until harvesting   Now I measure
drymustard   blackstrap molasses

and wonder who plants the beans
I soak overnight   Who gathers
them in   I close my eyes and see
Grandmother bent   stripping dried
pods   the light catching her hair

Gladyce Nahbenayash

Energy Exchanged

I saw you
In a room
Filled with the "White-Haired Ones"
In a wheelchair

We sat close
Energy exchanged
Through hands

Soft words came
To help
To encourage
To heal

As you sit courageously
With the bald eagles
On the Fourth Hill of Life

Fourth Hill of Life: In Ojibwa teachings, the time of aging. The earlier three hills are of infancy, adolescence and adulthood. For further explanation of this teaching, see Johnston, *Ojibwa Heritage*.

Charlene Blue Horse

Twenty Five or Fifty Cents

It's early spring in South Dakota, Pine Ridge Reservation. Tacin lives in the Day School housing with her grandchildren. It's Saturday, early May, and Sara has just driven through a blizzard to visit for a week.

Driving through the snow and wind, Sara has been thinking about her dragons sleeping while Tacín's furious Thunderbirds flapped their wings hurling the wind and swirling snow that will powder the earth's bottom like that of a baby's.

Sara has been thinking about all the opposites of this lovely land. Life beginning to paint the earth, color it with blooming plants of all sorts, the immediacy of death, a reminder of the smallness of life and the lack of immortality among humans. The wide spaces, rolling hills, prairie full of life that brings a sense of peace, harmony, wonder to this harsh and comforting land. The poverty, unrelenting as the land in this blizzard that tears families apart, fosters alcoholism and abuse among a people who prize harmony and compassion above all.

Tacín has been washing dishes, hanging out the wash, cleaning house, juggling the needs of the little people, going over the experiences of her California visit, and daydreaming her favorite dream.

Tacín dreams of building a lovely home out of a barn or renovating a century old house complete with cupolas and carved shining banisters that sweep down circular stairways. Her home would have skylights, lofts, an indoor sunken bathtub, blue, with a jacuzzi. A sunroom with so many plants it would resemble a jungle. The sunroom would double as a study and breakfast nook. She dreams of having enough land around her house to grow gigantic trees, a healthy sized garden, and horses, chickens, ducks and goats for the kids. She takes the time to add practical touches. A generator, well, windmill and her outhouse that would be an ode to Thomas Crapper.

Tacín knows that all this is dreaming. She knows that her kitchen, large and light with a built-in dishwasher and window seat by the wood stove would take lots and lots of money she would never have unless some relative she never heard of, or some forgotten client she had helped long ago, would suddenly bequeath a million or two to her. She dreams. She escapes that way. Dreams keep her going, give her hope, even if false. Maybe one of those contests she is always entering and never winning will pan out.

The blizzard has calmed, finally, to a light snow. Sara drives up to Tacín's house; the kids run to hug her. Seems like thirty wet little faces peeking out of snowsuits crowding around her, a thousand small rainbows form, calling out; "Auntie, Hi, Auntie."

A little dark girl, strands of hair peeking out from her hood, holds out a hand to catch snow drops while licking the other.

Sara follows Tacín's grandchildren, remembering Takoji, the name for grandchildren. She is thinking about similarities in the Lakota and Hebrew languages: the guttural sounds. Ina, Lakota for mother, Ema, in Hebrew. Father being Ate in Lakota and Aba in Hebrew.

"Unci, Grandma, Sara's here," they call out.

Tacín emerges from the kitchen.

"Put your stuff just anywhere, Sara. You made it. I was wondering how you'd do in this weather. You probably want honey with your coffee, right?"

"Sugar's O.K., Tacín."

"Good. I got commod honey. It's dark and runny. I don't really trust it. They probably mixed it with colored corn syrup. I know this white sugar's the pits, but the only drugs I get, are caffein and sugar and I can do them both at once."

Tacín pours "camp" coffee from her ever present blue and white speckled porcelain coffee pot. The phone rings.

"Hi, how ya doin'? No, I'm not going; I decided to stay home. I didn't want to leave the kids again after only a week at home. Sara's here for a visit.

"Anyway. . . . You're kidding me. Mathilda, Mathilda Peppercorn? I just saw her on my way to the airport two weeks ago. No, I picked her up outside of Mission. I thought she'd be on that road forever.

"Oh, God, who's doing it?. . . . They're lucky if they get fifty or a hundred dollars. When's the services, or are they having one?. . . . Doesn't she have a daughter?. . . . God, well maybe I can get down there; call me and I'll let you know and we can go together.

"Yea. Love to all. Yea, bye."

"Somebody you know died?" Sara asked.

Tacín gets the coffee and sits with Sara. The grandchildren come in dripping and red cheeked from the cold. Sara tells them to hang their snowsuits on the hooks on the backporch, quietly, so then won't wake the baby, and then they can play in their rooms or watch T.V.

"Yea, somebody I just saw two weeks ago died. An Elder lady. They found her this morning. She must have been out hitchhiking again, she was lying on the side of the road. I remember she kept wanting to get to Vermillion.

"I had just left the kids with my Son and Daughter-In-Law. I was on my way to the airport to fly out of Rapid to Alaska. As I turned off Highway 18, outside of Mission, on my way to Murdo, and the freeway, she was hitching there."

"So, did you pick her up?"

"Well. . . . "

"Did you know her family?"

"I wasn't going to pick her up. I knew she'd probably be drinking. She used to hang out in the post office to keep warm

31

in the winter. Always asking for twenty five cents or fifty cents. "She lost her husband years ago, maybe ten or twelve years. He died in a snowstorm just out of Valentine, trying to hitch a ride back to Mission, after the bars closed."

"Is that when she started drinking?"

"No. When her daughter was about eight or ten years old, or at least that's what I heard, she carried another baby full term, but her old man, drinking, had beat her and the baby was stillborn. Then it was one of those situations where the wife joins her husband, trying to drown her sorrows and ease the pain in booze."

The baby woke up and Tacín went to hold him. She knelt on the floor cradling him in her arms and softly cooing to him. Mato, her eldest grandson, brought her a diaper, and she changed and came back to sit with Sara for a few minutes again.

"Tacín, I'm really curious about Mathilda. What about the daughter?"

"Well, she was mentioning the daughter in the car. See, I saw her hitching out in the cold like that. Skinny little Mathilda, thin, dark print dress, long black worn quilted old coat with a big bottle hidden under it. The bottle was cradled like a baby under her right arm. She had her left thumb out. I passed her, but as I did, I knew she'd seen me and I didn't want to pick her up. You know I won't pick up drunks as a rule. I mean, if I don't know ahead of time, I just drop them off as soon as I get a good whiff.

"So, I passed her, but then felt guilty right away because she *is* an Elder, *you* know how we're raised to always respect Elders, and to make sure they are taken care of. That obligation to help? I stopped. I always did like her, but also felt sorry for her and you know I have this thing about being asked for money to buy booze."

"That's it? How far did you take her? What about her daughter?"

"Wait now. Let me check on the kids; they are too quiet."

Tacín put the baby down and started toward the hall. The baby grabbed her.

"Me want water, Mom."

"What, Takoja?"

"Me want water, míni, Mom."

"All right, just a second while I check on your brother."

"No, Mom. Me want water. Get it, then."

Tacín sort of slumped in resignation, went to the tiny B.I.A. kitchen, got him a glass of water half full, went back down the hall. The kids must have been up to something because Sara could hear Tacín speaking quietly but in a very firm voice to them while they were protesting something and trying to say the other one did it. Tacín came back, went into the kitchen, warmed up the coffee, and sat again. The baby came in and was hoisted up on her lap.

"Mato hurt my finger, Mom. Look, Mom, kiss it, my owwee."

"Oh, poor boy. Give me that finger, let me see it."

She looks at the finger and kisses it.

"There, my boy, all better. Go help clean up now."

"All right."

"God, Sara, sometimes when they go to bed, I just cry. Sometimes I'm so tired and they are being just little bummers. I think I'm just too old to be doing this again, so what I should do is throw them in the garbage can and hope for the best. Then I see them sleeping and they look like little angels. Sometimes I don't want to be bothered so I can visit, like now, but can't and then one comes with a kiss or hug or owwee, and I love them so hard. Maybe I need to find some unbreakable glass domes with little feeders and potties, so I could just place them on display like they used to do with statues of the saints."

"I know what you're saying, Tacín, I would have liked to have thought of that when mine were teenagers."

"Right, I remember those years. Maybe I still have time to save up for the domes; they're probably expensive."

"What about Mathilda, Tacín?"

"Oh, yeah, where was I? I picked her up. The sky was all gray and cloudy. It had been warm for a week, remember? Anyway, it was cold and looked like the Thunders were coming. I didn't have the heart to leave her on the road like that.

"She got in the car. The smell of booze began to over-whelm me. I asked where she was going.

"'Murdo,' she said; 'I'm trying to get to Vermillion to see my daughter. I'll get some money from my sister at Murdo, get on the bus to Vermillion. My niece is there, you know, they got a good school.'

"The smell was getting heavy, so I opened the window. She was sitting in the back, and I saw her look at my pipe, sneak the bottle down under her feet. I thought she must be getting worried about having that bottle, that *bad spirit* with her. Looking at the sky, I said, '*Heca wakiyanwan*. The Thunders are coming.'

"'Oh,' she said, 'I forgot you understand Indian.'

"Then she said something unintelligible or I didn't hear her. I said something like, 'What?' She repeated herself. I was overwhelmed by the smell, distracted. I thought she said she was going to be sick. You know, hungover. Then I remembered the unintelligible word, magaju, to rain. and knew she said it was going to rain. I answered, 'yes.' Then she really started talking Indian.

"She talked about how the farmers really needed rain because of the drought and the snow melt not being enough. I told her I'd just come back from North Dakota and the river was flooding and it was snowing again so their drought was over. She told me that she would stop at White River and get some money from her sister-in-law before getting on the bus to Vermillion. Then we started talking about being little on the reservation. Growing up when very few people ever drank. I talked about running and playing on the rolling hills with lots of cousins; but she said she only had a brother and they just asked relatives or friends for twenty five or fifty cents. I knew she was asking for money, but ignored it. I said we never did that. I told her that we were taught never to ask for money, added that everyone was poor anyway.

"We had arrived in White River. I saw her sneak the bottle back into her coat. She got out and invited me to come see her in her new apartment across from the post office where they didn't allow visitors."

"Did she ever get to Vermillion to see her daughter?"

"No. She never did get to Vermillion. Wouldn't hitch that way, 'cause she was afraid of hitching alone through Winner, and then further off the reservation, due to the violence drunk Indians have to endure. That's what she always said."

"How long since she's seen her daughter?"

"I just asked about her daughter on the phone. Seems that they took her away, long time ago. They put her in a foster home in Vermillion. The people adopted her a couple of years later, then moved away. No one knows where. That was before the Indian Child Welfare Act, so she was adopted by a non-Indian couple."

"So, now she died, and they can't even find the daughter to notify?" Sara asked.

"Yeah. It's funny, but in the car, she was talking about a friend who'd died recently, and she and some of her friends went around collecting twenty five cents or fifty cents and collected almost a hundred dollars to bury him.

"She isn't from Rosebud, her husband was, so the Tribe can't help with the burial. No relatives to be found. Some people, including the drunks, are going around collecting twenty five or fifty cents to bury her. She must have known that she wasn't going to be here much longer. Why else would she tell me about her mythical friend?

"Is the story worth that, Sara? Wanna give twenty five or fifty cents toward burial expenses?"

Tacín: Lakota (ta cheen) female deer.

Commod: government food commodities.

Mato: (ma toe), Lakota word for bear.

Charlene Blue Horse

The Fall

My blood runs white
As snow or silence.
This Earth Boy, four years
Aware of Whispers

Falls, screams my name.
I search for blood
Heart beating faster than drums

I remember white ferns on
Bathroom windows, silent
His whisper: "Tunkasila
Painted them there."

And whisper: "Hush
No blood. Kiss —
          All better.

Tunkasila: Lakota, (toon ka she la), Grandfather, common reference to the
Creator.

Rose Mary Robinson

Woman

And when I ask
 From whence becomes my strength,
The silence echoes from
 The depths within myself,
And I hear the strong reply.
My strength is mine because I share
 In this universe
No less and no greater than
 The highest mountain or
The smallest blade of grass.
I am a reed to yield and bend
 Beneath the winds,
Standing tall when the storm
 Is ended. I sway amid the rushes,
Drawing sustainance from the waters
 Of life, making transition from
Dark to light in harmony with that Earth
 Who mothers me.

Ellen Kort

Flute-Player

In the museum gift shop
in Albuquerque   an old man
touches hand-carved flutes
chooses one shaped
like a bird   I watch him
close his eyes   raise
the instrument carefully
in all four directions

His flute song plays along
my arm   chills the back
of my neck   Tendrilled
notes push against me
I want to walk away
but can no longer move
I breathe in the old man's
music   scent of crushed sage

juniper   a dog baying downriver
mountains with cheekbones of stone
A Navaho woman weaving rugs
afraid that threads can trap
a soul in the same way
sundown burns at Chaco Canyon
When the music ends   I touch

his arm   "This song" he says
"is for my friend who fell from
the mesa last week and died"
I leave the museum   drive
to Santa Fe   past canyons where
ravens fly free from cliffs
their shadows rising and falling
like the sweet thin wail of a flute

Jim Stevens

Song to Carry the Virgin Places
(Buffy Sainte-Marie, following the full moon of *Hayenehah*)

Wind comes rustling the flowers of her blouse
One night with black dawn being poured thru silk
And she is passing into the wind thorns
So old to have these faces dreaming upon the edge

It is the souls of all the women in Fourth World
Who have ever lived
Down among the stones crying as four hawks between
 mountains

Returned thru deepness of clouds
Returned thru deepness of clouds
Returned thru deepness of clouds
Returned thru deepness of clouds

Woman of Cree waters singing the leaves into Earth
Woman of Cree fire singing the feathers into Sky
Heyaaaa   Wilderness world is one moment giving birth
Throws back her head crying as the panthers of the Web

Then her people are passing across drums of this
    inner forest
Then her people are sewing the sharper blood of Thunder
Then her people are balancing along heartbeat of Good
    Dance

So the round of being who is Grandmother settles in
    the bones
So great Moon rising to the luminous house of our
    gathering

Hayenehah: (ha yen ee hah), Late Harvest Moon of the Seneca, falling in
September.

Fourth World: Can mean two different things. Here, Sainte-Marie, with
others, is referring to indigenous cultures of Earth, including Native-Americans as well as people such as the Saami of Finland. See the poem "I Dance
Around the Turtle's Back."

Web: referring to the relationship of all creatures, all life.

Ellen Kort

Medicine Woman

Your voice is flute music
Wild Born   Keeper of Words
you count each feather
know every stone leaf web
When you close your eyes
bones tremble   the skull's
socket names your shadow
Healer who drums thunder
from the sky   you know
what the old people know
Animals listen   Raven
calls you from the moist
dark belly of night
And you come   smelling
of sweet grass   burnt
sage   Root Woman   Maker
of Seasons   sunlight
sings from your throat
flowers open their medicine
bags   offer heart blood
of purple-red veins
shake their rattle of seeds

Charlene Blue Horse

After the Sweat

Grandfather Stone whispered me awake
Washed me new as this smiling
Sun that peeks through opening
Fourth flap.

My hair drips water, Sacred
My body glistens like diamonds
Of dew on new grass dancing.
Grandfather Stones whispered me awake.

Songs still spirit dance through my head.
They speak of Ceremony, Sacred
Mother Earth clings to my body
Wraps me. I am new-born, mom-secure.

I celebrate myself, Sacred.
I am woman, I am new, an unfurling
Leaf, I am Creation, bursting
Red flames. Grandfather Stones, Sacred
Still whisper me awake.

My songs pray for pity
My prayers sing for health
My songs are grateful

For this day, Sacred
For my sister, Leaf, reborn
For Mother Earth, her hugs, her tears
For Grandfather Stones
                    That whisper, "New day."

Michael J. Roberts

Fragments, Dance and Vision

Remember how in
an ancient book of sacred dances,
the dancers rose, each in
their time or as one,
knees bending and straightening
every one entering the great circle
in a new way,
like the raptor above
its prey
tracking the sun's path
moving in smaller spirals inside
that one great circle.

Remember how in
that dance before it
was frozen dead on
dead leaves —
one dancer became
the wind sighing through the grass
and another

the hawk high up
over the prairie weeds
and one danced
the sun's part
beginning the circle which
was all of these

Gladyce Nahbenayash

Aunt Marie's Visit

It was my twenty-second winter on the earth, and I was in my very first teaching assignment in Wausau. I lived in an apartment in the heart of the city, above the Vogue Dress Shop, with my roommate Sandy.

I was surrounded by parking lots, steel fences, sidewalks and roads that were cold and hard. I missed being by the healing waters of Lake Superior, the sandy beaches, the tree brothers and green growing relatives of the earth back home. I missed the smell of the big water and being close to the aura or presence of the Water Spirit.

One night I was awakened by the feeling that there was something or someone in my bedroom. I normally slept soundly throughout the night. As soon as my head hit the pillow, I was out. This time something woke me up. I opened my eyes, but couldn't see anything. Waiting, I couldn't hear anything either, yet there was a strong sensation that something was there with me in the room.

I quickly went for the light switch. With the lights on and my eyes wide open like an owl's scanning everything, I couldn't see anything there with me, yet there was a strong feeling that there was something there. I went through the apartment, room by room, turning on lights, looking for whatever that something or someone was. I even looked through Sandy's bedroom, and turned on all the closet lights, checking out every space. Nothing was found or seen, yet I still had this sense that there was someone or something there in the room with me.

I sat on my bed, trying to figure out what was happening, what was going on. I was trying to make sense out of the strong vibrations I was getting. I left my bedroom light on that night, and eventually fell asleep again.

The next day when I returned home from teaching school, there was a postcard from my Mom, who lived in Ashland, telling me that my Aunt Marie was very sick in the hospital and having a painful time with her diabetes. I stared at the postcard for a long time and started to think about her.

During my undergraduate studies at Northland College, I had worked as a nurse's aide at Trinity Hospital in Ashland. After work, I would stop at Aunt Marie's home to check on her to see how she was getting along. She had her hands full raising two teenaged grandchildren by herself.

She usually wore a plain cotton housedress and over that, a cotton floral patterned apron with a pocket. She also wore long brown cotton stockings on her legs. I remember her face was gentle and serene, it held a quietly thoughtful and caring message to everyone she met.

She would give me tea to drink and we would sit there together. Sometimes we wouldn't talk at all, but we would just sit and commune without words. We would just be. Together.

When my roommate came home that night, I told her the news I had received from my Mom, and said, "I think my Aunt Marie died last night." I explained to her what had happened the night before, when I was awakened by the vibrations sensed in my room. Sandy reacted with chills when I told her this. She is not an Anishanabe. For us, the Spirits are around all the time, and I had grown up hearing stories about them and I was told that we must not be afraid of the Spirits that come to us.

Sandy said it was eerie and that it scared her, and asked me not to talk about it anymore.

The next day I received a letter from my Mom, telling me that my Aunt Marie had died.

So then I knew.

I called my Mom and told her about my experience in the night. She explained that my Aunt Marie had visited me in her spirit form, had come to see me in Wausau when she left her body.

I had grown up hearing many of these spirit-centered accounts from my grandmother Theressa Buffalo Greene Webster, my mother Nettie Thomas, Mrs. Cedarroot, Mrs. Mustache, and many others. I had thought many times that they were coincidental happenings, but now I know differently. I thank you, Aunt Marie, for showing me.

Pamela Green LaBarge

Patience

Black brings pain
To Kanata-ke tonight,
Autumn rushing faster
Than freezing rain to snow.
I wish I had the patience
Of Chiefs who came before me.
Next year at this time
I'll be walking slowly.

Kanata-ke: (ga na da gi), Oneida name for Green Bay.

Charlene Blue Horse

Tractor

We have driven that road every day. Highway 18 out of Mission, on the way to Okreek. Rolling prairie, stones, a few trees, bushes, an occasional deer.

We talk or just drive, watch the colors on the horizon, listen to our hungry stomachs growl, maybe plan what to cook. Always, whatever is happening or not happening, it is there.

The plot of land is large and square and flat without the comfort of trees or bushes or flowers. It just sits there without moving, without growing old, without change or hurry, never busy. It stands out even more in the snow. There are no drifts, just an eerie quiet flat white for about a half mile north of 18, then the house, windows out, paint peeled off long ago. A small square house, about the size of the old Sioux Transitionals, wood weathered to a dull grey, and empty. About a quarter mile south of the house, a little west, the small green tractor, bright green, paint like new. That tractor hasn't moved for years. It just sits there wearing a sort of lonely grin, like a child's toy that's been left.

II

Sometimes you comment, "Must be a story there. Maybe some poor farmer never could make it. He tried for years and got nowhere, one day out on his tractor, had just had enough. Maybe he just got off that tractor and left, headed for California and a regular nine to five job."

This is South Dakota, 1980s, Rosebud Reservation. That bright spot of green tractor still stands there surrounded by white snow in winter and yellow prairie grass in summer.

The economy is bad,always has been for Indians on the reservation. During the Depression, the rich in cities were jumping out of windows, committing suicide because they had lost a bunch of spending money on the market. Dust from drought, swirled around farmers in the Mid-West, so they could go to California, but now California is overcrowded, ribboned with freeways and brown. Now, it's the farmers whose ancestors got the land from the government, or the people who have to tell them that they have lost all their family has had for generations to the government, 'cause even the banks are closing their doors. Now the farmers, having lost everything, have nowhere to go, so they use guns. They have nothing to leave their families, so they take them too. First the wife and kids, then dog, maybe a banker or neighbor before they drive off on a lonely dirt road to shoot themselves. No, this is worse than the Depression, and the green tractor looks new, shines like a child's lost toy on that flat ground covered with white snow.

III

They were a nice middle-aged couple, Agnes and Harry. They had both grown up on the Rosebud Reservation, went to St. Francis Indian School. Harry ran away from school in the sixth grade and they never made him go back. Agnes finished the eighth grade there. Years later, they married, were hard workers, never had any children, but lots of nieces and nephews. They were happy together, respectful and quiet and thrifty.

Anyway, the B.I.A. sold them a house. A small square wooden house they moved on to their flat piece of land without trees. Not one tree, but the land and the house were theirs. They fixed up that house real nice, and it was always neat and cheery.

Agnes kept trying to plant flowers, but they never went very well, they tried a few cedar trees, saplings, that died and everyone blamed it on the gumbo, so finally they were going to add to their income some by planting vegetables and get a big tree, cottonwood, growing. They bought a brand new, last year's model, bright and shiny, green tractor.

Agnes and Harry had bought that bright green tractor in late fall, before the new models came out and planned to wait until late spring, buy some sand and fertilizer and seed, just before their niece, Dottie came back.

Dottie had married that Walking Bear guy, but something had happened. They said he started drinking, said he beat her. Anyway, she left him and went to the city. They said that she had a hard time in the city, five years, but she came back. She couldn't go to her parents, so she came here, to her auntie and uncle, her second parents.

Agnes and Harry, the whole family, were so happy to have her back. They had worried so long. She was a bit skinny from life in that city, but her momma/auntie would fatten her up.

Dottie was helping with the house work, cooking, sewing quilts, doing beadwork, She seemed awful quiet, but not unhappy. The winter was cold and the snow was deep, no place to go really, no excitement like in the city, but Dot didn't complain. She was pleasant and smiled, kept herself busy and helpful when she wasn't sleeping.

Dottie slept alot at first. It was as though she hadn't slept the whole time she was gone. She drank in sleep like it was water from some far away oasis. Sometimes at night, they would hear her having a bad dream. It was as though she was wrestling or fighting with someone and sometimes one of them would go in to wake her because she was screaming and struggling in her sleep.

One night, Dottie started to scream and cuss and yell and it sounded like she was being thrown around. Agnes and Harry both jumped up and ran to her. Dottie was awake and falling on the bed like she was being pushed, and her nose was bleeding. They lit the oil lamp and spoke gently, quietly to her.

"He came right in here Momma, he just wouldn't stop. He was trying to kill me. Oh God, help me, oh help me, Momma, you and Uncle, don't leave me, he'll come back."

Agnes put a cold rag on her nose to stop the bleeding and noticed that her eye and cheek seemed to be swelling.

"Who was it?" Agnes asked, but Dottie was crying and babbling and shivering, so they talked to her real calm.

"There was no one here, Dot, it was just a dream (they did wonder how she could be thrown by a dream), don't you worry now, we're right here, we won't leave you, won't let anything happen."

Those dreams had happened a couple of times before and she had had a bruise or two the next day but it really hadn't been that bad before tonight, so they hadn't said anything to anyone, just thought she'd had some bad experience in that city and needed time to heal. This time, Dottie had a black eye like she'd been socked with a fist, her lip and cheek were swollen and by the time she finally calmed down enough to pour coffee, her hands were still shaking.

Harry moved Dottie's mattress into their room, next to the bed. They noticed that Dot didn't sleep that night. She lay there just staring up at the ceiling. She would turn and toss, but she wouldn't get up. They decided to tell the relatives, discuss bringing the Medicine Man for ceremony. They had planned a dinner on Saturday, right there, so they would talk with the family then.

On Saturday, Harry got up early, built the fire, took the table and benches outside while Agnes and Dottie cooked soup and fry bread and made coffee. The women baked cakes, joked around some, Dottie seeming relaxed, Harry puttered around in the yard, started the tractor up and drove it around.

It had been a long and lonely winter. This was early spring and the snow had just melted. It was a beautiful warm and still morning, an occasional bird flew over and the sun shone. Harry could almost hear the leaves on that cottonwood he was going to plant and see the ripe vegetables sitting in the garden come late summer. This was going to be the first family gathering of the year.

Everyone arrived with more food and lots of winter stories and laughter. Cousins, aunts, uncles, parents, grandparents, new babies. A relative would sometimes glance at Dottie's black eye, but no one had asked about it.

After eating all that food, kids were off playing games, laughing and shrieking and the adults were settling down to quiet joking and visiting, keeping a close eye on the babies. Dottie had gone in the house for a nap.

Dottie's mother, father, and brother Nelsen cornered Agnes and Harry.

"How's Dottie been doin'—Has she been runnin' off—Has she been drinkin' or gettin' in fights—how's she been?"

They started to tell the family about the strange dreams Dot had been having, but suddenly, a strong wind swept through the flat yard and the house erupted.

Dottie was screaming. Blood curdling screams and there was a violent banging, you could almost see the walls bending from the blows. She was yelling and cussing and screaming finally, for help. Everyone was frozen to the ground for a few minutes, then they started running towards the house. The men ran in, telling the women and children to wait outside in case there was danger. The noise and racket seemed to stop just as Dottie's uncle and dad started in the house.

The women stood outside, silent, frozen, full of fear. They could hear the men cry out, "Oh no,—Oh God, no—."

Tears started to roll down their cheeks but their feet couldn't move. Nelsen kept hollering, "Don't come in here, don't come in."

After what seemed like an eternity to the women, but probably about ten or fifteen minutes, Harry carried Dottie out, wrapped in a red blanket. She had been beaten to death, but no one was in the house except her.

"A Spirit," Harry said, and the wailing and disbelief began. They sent Nelsen and two of his cousins to bring the Medicine Man. They brought him back there a couple of hours later. He looked at Dottie, lit some sage and sweet grass, took Nelsen with him and went in the house praying.

When they came out, the Medicine Man prayed and cleaned everyone off. He told them that a bad spirit had entered the house and killed Dottie. He said that they should leave the house, never come back except to care for the place once a year. Leave everything there. He said they should begin preparations for the wake.

IV

Earlier, Harry had been out showing off his brand new green tractor to his nephews, proud and laughing. Now the tractor sat in the front, the house no longer neat and clean and cheery, but broken and silent, as silent as his niece, Dottie.

What happened there, happened years ago. Now, once a year, Harry takes a few of his sisters and nieces over, they burn some sage and cedar, maybe some sweet grass, smudge the house down, put up new red tobacco ties for offering, protection, quickly clean and check the trunk to see if the family stuff is still there. The windows are gone, but they clean and pray.

Harry goes out to his tractor while they clean. He washes and shines the tractor until the sun bounces off that green paint, making it look like an earth star, brighter than day, small as a toy. Then he sits on that seat and daydreams that nothing had ever happened. He and Agnes are looking out the window of their neat and cheery house, smiling at their beautiful garden almost ready to harvest and the tractor resting under the shade of the cottonwoods.

That house and tractor still sit there. The tractor looking like a lost and lonely toy. The seasons pass and Harry goes by now and then, to shine his bright green tractor.

Part III

TEACHING AND PRAYERS

In this third section, we have placed poems and short stories which have to do with going into the Sacred Space which is at the center of all the creatures of the world. This Space is known as the Place of Silence. One finds this omnipresent center through learning from Elders and ultimately through communication with the Spirit-Helpers who are all around us in Mother Earth.

In "Language of the Birds," Gladyce Nahbenayash speaks of learning the ways of the world through the spirit-keepers of nature. Understanding this quality of life begins in carrying the presence of "wilderness." In Native-American words, this means the pristine places upon Earth.

Andrew Connors, in "Like the Snowflake," writes of a grandfather who is communicating his wisdom about the passage and the movement of life.

Pamela LaBarge's "The Moon Bear" is a poem about a vision which brings her the gift of a spirit-helper.

In "Vision Seeker," Ellen Kort writes of learning who you are as a person thru the dream-vision.

Gladyce Nahbenayash, in her poem "Keys," writes of the closedness of material world, and of the mysteriousness that a person encounters in working to transcend it.

In "Those Things That Come To You At Night," Kimberly Blaeser writes of the space of deep thought in which one finds the rhythms of ancient naturalness coming through Mother Earth.

"Cochiti Buffalo Dance" is Ken Metoxen's meditation upon the difficulty as well as the gifts of walking the spirit-path.

In "Let Me Be A Light" Mary Ann Doan prays her thoughts for purity and oneness of purpose.

Gladyce Nahbenayash in "Overland Skiing" describes the purification brought about through the natural world of winter.

"I Dance Around the Turtle's Back" carries Jim Stevens' appreciation of the eternal way brought about by Peacemaker, who is prophet and founder of Irokwa cultural system.

"Two Sections from a Short Longhouse Thanksgiving Offering" is Michael Roberts' translation of the opening of a Irokwa Longhouse prayer. This is the Irokwa wisdom way.

Charlene Blue Horse in "Wagluh' TaTapi" writes of the special offering which expresses a balance and reciprocity between spiritual souls.

In "The Giveaway," Mary Anne Doan expresses the power known among the Dakota peoples as *Wakan*, among the Anishinabe as *Manitou*, and among the Irokwa as *Orenda*. All these words mean simply a mystical oneness with the world.

In "Camping With Our Relatives" Gladyce Nahbenayash writes of some moments which led her to thoughts of Mother Earth and her creatures (of which humans, the two-leggeds, are but one). The poem is about the ability to communicate, one creature and another.

"aniishinaabe song," in Rose Mary Robinson's words, speaks to the four races of humans, the two-leggeds, and how creation began in harmony with Mother Earth.

Closing this section, the poem "Truckers say they" is Ken Metoxen's calling out to European-Americans and other non-indigenous peoples, the younger brothers and sisters of Turtle Island (our hemisphere), for understanding in the ancient ways.

Gladyce Nahbenayash

Language of the Birds

Spring 1953
Backyard cool green grass under pubescent limbs
Warm fluffy jumping kittens dart
Around Mrs. Moustache their mother

Grandma watching
From behind screened kitchen door
Apron pocket holding pouch tobacco
For her pipe

Said it was time
To go out in the woods
To be alone to pray to fast
To learn the language of the birds

Necessary for my be-ing
A proper way to walk
Her advice hung there in space for twenty-five years
Until I went to the woods alone.

Andrew Connors

Like the Snowflake

Sara and Justin enjoyed walking with Grandpa. They'd walk everywhere, in the malls, the halls, the used car lots, electronic wish shops, the parks, everywhere. And when they walked, they talked. They talked about many things, Sara, Justin, and Grandpa did. They talked about everything, and sometimes talked about nothing. Today they walked through the park, on a bright, breezy fall day, talking about life.

Sara and Justin were different today. Grandpa sensed this. Their usual bounce was now a memory overburdened with complex adolescent thoughts. "Another rough night, last night," Grandpa asked?

Sara nodded. Justin moped along, head down. "Sometimes kids can be so cruel," she said.

"Sometimes Mom and Dad just don't understand," Justin added.

"That a fact," Grandpa chimed.

Sara contined, "My friends make me so mad. One minute they're your friends, then they're talking behind your back."

"I can't get them to believe me about anything," Justin remarked. "Told Mom I was hanging around the model store and had nothing to do with Mrs. Baxter's window gettin' busted."

A snowflake fell lazily by.

"Sally wanted me to go with her to the mall and meet boys," Sara said. "I went, but I really wanted to stay home and read."

"Then there was that time when Dad thought I left the stereo running all night," Justin said. "Talked to me about electric bills, and gas bills and food and on and on. I didn't leave the stereo on." He glanced at Sara. "I don't listen to no Michael Bolton."

"No, you listen to that head banger nonsense," Sara sniffed.

Two snowflakes danced in the air while an ice crystal symphony played, floating by. Grandpa watched the ballet, thinking about his youth in another time and place. They were playing crack the whip on the river, Snow Dancer on the end, he the head. Pop, he cracked that whip and old Snow Dancer snapped off the end, sailing down the frozen river carpet towards a mammoth snowbank.

"I don't know what anyone wants from me," Sara said. "Sometimes I want to do what I want to do. I don't know why Sally and them always want me to do other things. Just want to get me in trouble."

"All I want is to know what they expect of me," Justin added. "I do what I'm supposed to do. Sometimes I wonder why I'm here."

"Why is a snowflake here," Grandpa asked. They looked at him like kids do when an adult says something completely out of context with what they wanted to hear. You know, a duh?

"Why, it's snowing," they squealed, finally noticing the simple cascade of ice crystals around them. "It's so pretty," Sara said. "It won't stick," Justin observed, watching the flakes touch earth and disappear. "I'd hate to be a snow flake," he said.

"I don't know," said Sara, catching a flake on the tip of her mitt. "They're so beautiful."

They stopped and watched the snow fall, lost in thought with the drama floating around them. And Grandpa smiled, they were so much like the seasons.

This smile didn't go unnoticed by Sara and Justin. Why you smiling Grandpa, they asked. "Just rememberin'," Grandpa answered. Rememberin' what, they wanted to know. "How we're so much like the snow," Grandpa said.

Like the snow, they laughed.

Like the snow.

How so? Sara was intrigued by the mystique of momentary beauty floating in the sky. That beauty would live forever in the endless world of her mind. Justin was repulsed by the idea of a slushy snow being trampled on by people and cars and buses and snowplows. Here today, gone tomorrow.

"Think of the snowflake," Grandpa began. "Do you think that just because the seasons change, or it melts when it touches the earth that it doesn't have a purpose?"

"Has crossed my mind," Justin remarked.

"I don't know," Sara said. "But I don't see how we're like snowflakes."

"Oh, but we are," Grandpa said. "Think about it. Like each of us, snowflakes have their own unique design. Creator has a sense of beauty, you know. No two things are the same. Yet these individual, unique, snowflakes are part of a greater community, the community of snow."

"The community of snow," they laughed.

"Oh yes," Grandpa smiled. "That single snowflake is born in the collective good of Mother Earth. Given shape and form by the parents and grandparents of the four elements, earth, water, fire, and sky. Each contributed to that snowflake's birth, and each has a responsibility to see that snowflake through to its ultimate purpose."

"Now what purpose could a snowflake ultimately have," Justin wanted to know.

"And how does that make us like snowflakes," Sara did too.

"The snow covers the earth while she sleeps," Grandpa said. "And though the snow is made of millions of snowflakes, each with their own unique designs, the snow community knows that its purpose is to replenish our Mother while she sleeps. And it may seem to you that the snowflake melts and fades away, but think of this, does it really fade away?"

"No, it becomes water," Sara chirped brightly.

"Or slush," Justin said.

"Water or slush," Grandpa laughs, "it changes and grows, and moves into the world seeking its ultimate destiny. It feeds our Mother and becomes part of an even greater community. It becomes the plants, animals, the birds, fish, us. Then after its worldly purpose has been served, it returns to the sky from which it came, watching with interest as its offspring, the generations to follow, repeating the cycle started long before individual snowflakes were born. And as the seasons change, so does that flake, until finally it's ready, descending to the earth with a new design, a new name, yet still a part of the greater whole."

"Yeah, well," Sara stuttered.

"But I don't see how that makes us like snow flakes," Justin said.

"Well," Grandpa began, "life ain't easy for that snowflake. Oh no. On the way down it had the wind to contend with. On the ground other snowflakes, then it moves into Mother Earth, with a whole new bunch of things to contend with."

"So . . . you're saying that like us, snowflakes deal with nasty things just as we do, but it has a purpose to fulfill, just like we do," Sara said smartly.

"Sounds like a crock," Justin sneered. "I still don't know what my purpose is. I'm only ten years old."

"You will, someday. Anyhow, it's a thought," Grandpa said, as they wandered through the snow.

It's just a thought.

Pamela Green LaBarge

The Moon Bear

Moon
Inside me rises.
Moonlight
Knows the way
Into the
Holy Cavern.
Crayfish float
Reflectingly
In pools,
They sing
Of ghosts
Inhabiting this cave.

At cavern's heart
Faint light is seen.
A glowing plant
Grows wildly
Out of a pond.
Moon Bear
Waits

And feasts upon
The luminous blooms.
They say
What is needed to know.
And Moon Bear, in turn,
Tells me.

Ellen Kort

Vision Seeker

Once you were eagle
bending the shape
of sky   Once you were
scar etched in pale
blue flesh   Windroar
Shadow-clustered
feathers beating
the drum of air   This
is how a man finds
his name in the circle
of fire   thin slice
of moon   shoulder
of wingbone   in fingers
that curl like talons

Gladyce Nahbenayash

Keys

When people leave this world
And journey to the spirit
They leave many keys
Behind
That remain mysterious
For us to puzzle over

I too
Carry many
Sometimes not remembering
What they open

Some keys of the past
Their importance
Forgotten

Present keys open
Certain buildings, doors, file drawers
Cars, apartments and homes
Carefully attached to portfolio,

Purse, pockets
Or placed carefully under a mat

Metal keys
Important in this world
But not useful to open
Or enter the next

Kimberly Blaeser

Those Things That Come
to You at Night

"Old Woman, Grandmother," she said. "They come to me at night."
"What is it they want?"
"Can't tell. Ain't like I really hear them clear."

Like voices I've known
sounding off
over the hill
behind the milk shed
under the belly of a car
coming through the woods
familiar tones and rhythms
like surface conversation
heard while underwater
the sliding pitch of sound
but no clear word borders.

"You must try to hear and remember. Sounds, pictures, the stories
they bring you, the songs."

Swimming among the fluid notions
of dream space
where voices land
in the hollow behind the house
and echo back to sleeping souls
where ideas ricochet
off of each documented waking moment
but strike home
in the slumbering core.

*"They tell me things I'm sure. I want to get up to follow. But
I can't pull my body along. When I wake up I am homesick
for those voices. And then sometimes, maybe when I am
hauling water or frying bacon, I remember something,
just a feeling really."*

*The old woman, bent over her basket, nods her head slowly.
"Yes," she says. The younger one waits. Nothing more.*

Night speaking
touching spirit
without distinguishable words or voice
calling by name
calling your ancient being
arousing that felt destiny
waking all past
folding the torn moments together
and shaking them out whole.

"Grandmother?"
*"It's that way, child.The night things. Like how you learned to walk.
Nobody can teach you."*

Now a rumbling comes
heard over a heartbeat
beating more rapidly
with a fear of
greatness
felt in the bladder

breathed with flared nostrils
approaching like a flood
it rushes upon you
cleanses you with night desire
leaves you floating peacefully
into daylight.

"They get louder, I'm told."
"The voices?"
*"Ayah. Louder if you don't seem to hear. Louder still until you
hear or go deaf. Everybody has a choice you know. Some go night
deaf. Others learn to listen."*

Singing the songs
of midnight
going quiet, smiling shyly
when someone hears
listening inside
voices rounding each corner
of yourself
forming you
from dark night
remembering
those things
that come to you at night.

Kenneth Brickman Metoxen

Cochiti Buffalo Dance

All of this I leave for you
Everything I have I shake off and leave
for you
Corn Maiden
Antelope
Sheep
Deer
Buffalo
Protector
And medicine men.
With your gift to share my throat begins
to tense with eyes straining to remain
clear
My Pueblo brothers and sisters, as tears
begin to swirl in my soul, I give
you my heart in exchange of my gift
to you for looking at me but once.
As you all leave once again from this
World, from your fast, a special part
of my heart leaves with you.

While I walk the tenseness and strain-
ing, upon my spirit also walk.
This content pain steers another path,
although, I am told
Corn Maiden
Antelope
Sheep
Deer
Buffalo
Protector
And Medicine men
Along with contentment
Will all return next year to my heart
I will wait for you all my friends

Cochiti: the pueblo nation of the Southwest.

Mary Anne Doan

Let Me Be a Light

Let me be a light
Not the faint flicker
Of the firefly,
But a bold beacon
Like the Morning Star
Shining high
Illuminating the path ahead.

Let me be a Song
Not the sharp staccato
Of the cricket's chirp
But a rapturous melody
Like the meadowlark's merry voice
Bringing joy to the world
In each harmonious note.

Let me be a Prayer
Not the sad lament
Of the mourning dove
But the strong reverent petition

Of the eagle's beating wing
Carrying each loving bequest
Skyward to the Creator

Let me be all these
That I might serve
My purpose well
Upon this gentle planet,
And be blessed in the blessing
Of all my brothers and sisters
Touched by my Light, my Song, my Prayer.

Gladyce Nahbenayash

Overland Skiing

With movement forward
A prayer is offered
To Gitchie Manito
Each glide finds
New strength
Hope
Fresher spirit

Ears fill with
The clean sound of silence
Forest fresh oxygen
Enters lungs
Blood
Brain
While my eyes capture
The pure white sculptures
Of the Wind Spirits

Overland skiing brings
Lightness of spirit
Heart
Purification of mind
Cleansing of physical being
From inside out

Miigwetch Gitchie Manito
For air
Silence
Life movement

Gitchie Manito: (gee chee man ee toe) Ojibwa word for Great Spirit.

Miigwetch: (mee gwetch) thank you.

Jim Stevens

I Dance Around the Turtle's Back

(For Oren Lyons, from his speaking)

On this day, the last day of the Fourth World
I hold fast in my heart the Great White Pine
How the Eagle perches atop, so blood courses thru the Tree
Eagle screams and the leaves share their green

Down these eight paths turns the Law
And all is right
Beginning and Ending in the eye of flight

I am part of these words and know how Peacemaker
Sat in the woman's house for she fed the wayfarers
Cleansed all the tears from the man who saw Thought
Then a song of birds turned all snakes to right power

The mountain continuing on
The river continuing on
The breath continuing on
The rock continuing on

Who speaks the words keeps the beautiful house in order
In these images know everything becoming heartberry
I live this day and it is the only day I live

Seven generations going before this day
Seven generations coming from the body

The central fire in the Council of Good Minds
Singing into life something which always walks beside

And at daybreak, a sound of the hand clapping
Red so deep it is a good day to pass thru
Seeing the Sun come up in the same place it always has
Knowing this truth in the Circle of the World

To carry belief in the People
To carry belief in the Ceremonies
To carry belief in the Earth

I hand you this bowl for within it the blood of all souls
Always thru the Grandmothers and the Grandfathers
On four days these voices coming to pass

One to sing
One to dance
One to speak
One to listen

Here is where I greet you.
Nyahweh Sganoh.

Fourth World: Here, in Irokwa usage, refers to a stage of learning of The People. All cultures possess similar stages, but depending upon the culture, there are varying degrees of awareness of this development.

Great White Pine: Among The Irokwa, people of the Longhouse, who traditionally refer to themselves as Hodenoshonee, Pine refers to the Great World Tree, upon which all creatures live.

Law: Great Law of Peace of Hodenoshonee; the governing principles, the Constitution.

Peacemaker: The great Huron spiritual teacher, whose true name is never spoken outside of formal council, who brought The Great Law and united the original nations of Hodenoshonee (Mohawk, Oneida, Onondaga, Cayuga and Seneca). Around 1750, Tuscarora Nation joined this body.).

Council of Good Minds: the governing body of traditional Irokwa.

Nyahweh Sganoh: (nya weh sga noe) traditional greeting of Irokwa people, meaning literally "thank you for the Great Peace."

Michael J. Roberts

Two Sections From a Short Longhouse Thanksgiving Offering

Now we're together.
There are many of us,
many of the people.
A few more of our people
are still coming in.
We will find the words
and together as we were taught
joined in one voice
offer thanks.
If only two people come
together in this manner,
their shared words will be holy —

and the first thing we must sing of
is how we may best carry
this happiness to all people.

Now, as though of one heart,
we call out to one another
in one voice,
with one mind.

And now let's talk about the Earth,
the Creator's gift,
who is our Mother
as we are her children —
All that is good in our lives comes from her!
Her love is the fruit hanging in the trees,
which have in their making solace and power.
Many trees together are the forests standing forever.
Everything we see around us comes from the Creator.
So that we may live good lives.
And the Creator made river running fast and slow.

Some are great torrents and some trickles.
And the lakes, some of them are giants,
lakes that are worlds.

All of these things are of the Earth
and are her strength in her turnings.
Now for all the Earth's gift's to us
those many things which fill us so well
we hold her close and thank her.

Charlene Blue Horse

Wagluh' TaTapi

For Joe Eagle Elk,
who told the story of how the
"Spirit Plate" offering, the prayer
before the meal, began.

I
Soft winds blow cold
Carry the laughter of relatives
Little people learning age
Wild flowers skip across
The prairie.

Smoke snakes through the air
Like thin mist
Sweeping stories past camp

II
Grandmother, her hair white
As smoke
Smells the sweet aroma

Frying meat that sings and dances
On the hot
Coals.

Grandmother, hair white like dream
Face mapped with love
Speaks of hunger, relatives, children
Grandchildren.
The green leaf is curled around the meat
The tallow.

III

"Pila maye daughter, I give you the gift
Of prayer. Over the mountain
Into the valley
Near the singing trees
Buffalo, a slow herd
Waits.

Remember me, my children
Grandchildren.
You will receive the gift
Of the four leggeds
Bellies will grow round.
Mitakuye Oyasin."

Grandmother, gone like smoke
Or dream
Gone like wind
Like green leaves in winter.

IV

Frost powdered the prairie white
Silent like smoke
They slip into the whispering valley
Arrows sing in the cold wind.

Uncle carries the green leaf
Wrapped like a blanket

Meat and tallow dripping
Steam curling into the air.

He gives thanks and asks
For what is needed.
We will remember grandmother
With the first of our food
With prayers like
Song.

                    V
Grandmother came before the pipe
Listens now
To little people learning age
Prayer that snakes through air
Like white smoke.
We still pray
That way.

Pila maye: (pee la my aye), thank you.

Mitakuye Oyasin: (mee tak oo ya seen) Lakota words for "All My Relations."

Mary Anne Doan

The Giveaway

In the Moon of Grass Appearing
    I am full
    Full
    with
    LIFE
Ringing through me
The threads of Skan
Connecting me
To every bursting bud
Slip of sweet clover
Dandelion, daffodil
And rows of rooted ones
Dressed in sacred green.

In the Moon of Grass Appearing
    I am full
    Full
    with
    JOY
Singing through me
The threads of Skan
Connecting me

With every symphony
Blown upon warm southern winds
Chirped by spring peepers
Warbled by winged ones
And echoed merrily in each river
Running fast and free.

In the Moon of Grass Appearing
    I am full
    Full
    with
    AWE
Sweeping through me
The threads of Skan
Connecting me
With every romping colt
Skipping lamb
downfilled duckling
Each mother and newborn
Bonding in Birth's miracle

In the Moon of Grass Appearing
    I am full
    Full
    with
    LOVE
Racing through me
The threads of Skan
Connecting me
With Mother Earth
Father Sky
The two-leggeds, four leggeds, Creepy crawlies, wingeds
rooted ones, the little people and those of stone.
And I open my heart
That I may be part
Of the Creator's loving Giveaway.
In the Moon of Grass Appearing.

Skan: (pronounced with nasalized *n*, shkan) in the cosmology of the Dakota
Nations, the Spirit of Sky.

Gladyce Nahbenayash

Camping with our Relatives

Inside our orange pup tent
Lying close to our Mother Earth
Drawing in her strength and energy

Be still my Granddaughter . . .
Feel our Mother Earth breathe
With each breath she gives energy to us

Shhh . . . listen my little one
Listen to the tree people . . .
They are talking to us
When you are very quiet you can
Hear their message

Listen to the water spirits
At the pebbled shore lapping
Our Grandmother Moon with her soft light smiling
Many star brothers and sisters above us guiding

My Granddaughter and I
Camping with all our relatives
Her black eyes shining.

Rose Mary Robinson

aniishinaabe song

red and yellow
    black and white,
        stretch the shadows,
water mirror'd magic
plays the scattered music
        of the earth.
melody of colors
    reaching deeply,
        mem'ry of another time
when we belonged
as perfectly as shadow
        to the sun.
how simply does
    the list'ning reach
        to blended waters,
ev'ry word a floating leaf
        upon the waves.

Aniishinaabe: (ah nee shin ah bee) The People, who are often referred to as
Ojibwa, Potawatami, Ottawa and Cree.

Kenneth Brickman Metoxen

Truckers say they
                hear that
                        long
        highway
Callin'

        Why then
            can't
    others understand
                                our
Callin'
        The Wind,
                    Fire,
                        Sky,
    land of the rising sun
                where the mysteries
    Come   direction of the old
    Ways   and the
                        humble seasons

        Why?
            Because their own
    ears have been snipped by
    their own devil, not ours
    We never had a hell. Still don't

Part IV

TALKING INDIAN

The pieces of this last grouping have at their root an inner knowing of the Self as Native-American. But at the same moment in these poems and stories, there is the sense of being tested within that knowledge, while still holding to the center of one's being. These pieces are placed in our closing section because they mirror the place of indigenous people at this moment in time: as living in the midst of a dominant material culture while still understanding the People's true place as spiritual beings who shall balance Sky and Earth. There is the sense of a long civilized history left ignored.

Kimberly Blaeser's "Meeting Place" recreates the memories of sharply different sights while emerging from a small lake of northern Wisconsin. One is of her placid childhood, the other is of seeing on the boat landings the unbalanced faces of young people.

"The Plumed Snail" is Jim Stevens' meditation on the civil events of 1994 Mexico in their proper perspective as the culmination of ancient spiritual movement on Turtle Island.

In the poem "Indian Talk," Charlene Blue Horse recreates a discussion of the imbalances wrought through pressures from the dominant culture.

Michael Roberts' "Maybe I Should've Worn a Feather" is about the coarseness of attitude often encountered by Native-Americans in their daily lives.

"Living History" is Blaeser's ironic turn on the perceptions often encountered by Native-Americans: that of themselves as "living fossils."

Blue Horse's "Poem For Our Ancestors Dedicated to the Kiwanis Club," is of the spiritual disrespect, ignorance, and lack of understanding held by people new to Turtle Island and uninvested in her ways.

"When" by Rose Mary Robinson is a call for compassion in our present-day world.

"On the Way to the Chicago Pow-Wow," Kimberly Blaeser, is about the chaos and disorder of modern world.

Blue Horse's "Feeling Watched" recreates a sense of the harassment felt by many Native-Americans as we simply go about trying to live our lives; of the pressures brought about through events such as came about at Wounded Knee, at 1970s Pine Ridge, and Wisconsin's St. Alexian Novitiate. These are events imposed by a government and society which itself exists in a terrible fear, thus invoking violence as a means of escape from itself.

"Niimi's Song: Traveling Thunder" by Andrew Connors is a song praying that the dominant culture of America shall be able to become free of the material box in which it finds itself. It is about a lack of vision brought about through a critical starving of the senses.

"Whitefish Bay" is Ken Metoxen's singing of the circle of indigenous dancing and song which is a center of Native-American being. The poem recreates the sights and sounds of a contemporary powwow.

Kimberly Blaeser

Meeting Place

Sweet garments of memory,
I don't know how to follow you.

Crossing and recrossing
the borders.

I was a mermaid once
for ten minutes
in a four-year-old's eyes
and became one
then
and now
when I remember
and emerge.

From the water
laughing
hair like seaweed.

Crowned princess, twice
one night in North Carolina

one in Illinois
my identity
so easy
Indian princess
the one in Peter Pan.

Refuses
like him
to grow old.

Simple distances those.

But these.

At the boat landings, I see you raise your leg, knee bent, stepping to shore. Your hair falls across my eyes. I tilt our chin and flick it back, then brush it away with the back of our hand because the fingers hold to the handle of the bucket. The hand is chapped and tight with the cold night air. It smells of fish.

Then you look up and I see you grin your triumph. I remember the tired joy we felt at bringing home a meal. But when we look up, we see the game warden who took those fish we netted that hungry year. We zip up our thin jackets and rub our hands against our pant legs knowing we must try again and knowing he knew, too.

I pass the bucket to the eager children, reach down to grab the boat and pull her further onto shore. The old man grasps the other side, together we ease it out of the water. But as I turn to nod my thanks, shouting faces, angry twisted mouths, crowd in at the edges of the night. They are that frowning game warden of forty years past. They are the resort owners' overgrown children, cursing, throwing stones.

You are stepping out of the boat. Your hair falls full across your eyes. When you push it back, I am standing before you, a protector. You are my past, standing before me. I am at the landing, one foot on shore, one in the shallow water.

Jim Stevens

The Plumed Snail

There came the moment when the world was changing over. I was placing words on a spiral as it was circling ever down into the Earth. I was attending the words closer to the center when the thought came to rearrange the words, so that they would turn in the opposite direction. There would be a motion for them to circle into the Sky.

My hand was there placing the words in a different order from where they had been. A different logic had settled from which I had surely been accustomed. The words were arranging themselves always closer to the center when they became glyphs, pictures and forms.

Now the circle grew from south to east. The words were sorting themselves into a long house. My hand put down the green, yellow and red face, which had closed eyes. This was so small, and fashioned in jade. And at the very eastern door, deep in that center, there was my name placed, as in a signature, so the Grandmothers and Grandfathers would know this a gesture hidden in my ribs.

> *The impending Sun is*
> *Taking lodge in the heart*

The impending Sun is
Taking lodge in the heart

The impending Sun is
Taking lodge in the heart

The impending Sun is
Taking lodge in the heart

When I opened my eyes, I was thinking of all the world's dying which was wafting into our bodies. This was its special season, I thought. I switched on the television and there was news of the Mexican presidential candidate Colosios who had died after being shot yesterday in Tijuana.

Bullets that were not words, they were thoughts balanced on a rocky ledge, had smashed into his body. That was on the day a wave came from Field of Plenty to sweep things away. Today was a day of going around the circle, the day he passed over. The Death of rulers was emerging out of the head of our week.

These two eyes are
Setting fire to the night

These two eyes are
Setting fire to the night

These two eyes are
Setting fire to the night

These two eyes are
Setting fire to the night

I remembered what had taken place several weeks before. The Bear Woman and I had gathered wood for a fire. We had constructed the pyre with a peak at the top and lighted the edifice. It was the coldest night of the year. During the next hour, the fire was extinguishing itself with ever so exquisite slowness. At the end I was seeing with only the Spirits of the Darkness as my guides.

And I am living with this as a vision of the death going on all around me, the dying over our world. The breath comes from the other side of the veil. It is transformed into Wind. It is not imparting itself to the fire. There is a new fire being born somewhere, elsewhere, anywhere but here.

These eight winds turning as
Serpent arching her back

These eight winds turning as
Serpent arching her back

These eight winds turning as
Serpent arching her back

These eight winds turning as
Serpent arching her back

Now the thoughts come of Sub-Commandante Marcos, who deep in Chiapas wears the balls of his feet in the fight against hunger and death. Grieve for the healer who goes away past the rock. Cry long with Red Brother and Sister. The Mayan warriors are coming down from the mountains and renewing the struggle. They instituted this path on First of January. Their day is in the bones for the Old Ones of the forest.

Hunahpu and Ixbalamque, the companions who have long tails and are able to pass like a whisper from tree to tree, are reawakening Possum and beginning the ball-game in the underworld against the Lords of Death.

I remember the true-people of the southern lands come into their own in the days of Feathered Serpent returning. Sub-Commandante says that he is not Commandante, for he is responsible to the council of elders. The elders are responsible to Feathered Serpent. Who is Commandante?

The Fourth World at the last
Willing her paws through the crack

The Fourth World at the last
Willing her paws through the crack

The Fourth World at the last
Willing her paws through the crack

The Fourth World at the last
Willing her paws through the crack

So are these words being passed in an unending circle.
They are always in two paths to the center. One goes deep into
Mother Earth. One goes far into Father Sky. Everything which
occurs in the world is the Plumed Snail who moves so slowly
as she eats all the filth of the world.

Agegenh   Agondadonh
This is shaking the smoke
The dreaming Red Willow branch
I am seeing

Hunahpu & Ixbalamque: (hoon ah poo, ish ba lom kwe) the twin creators
of the Mayan world.

Feathered Serpent: the great teacher-prophet of Mesoamerican peoples.

Agegenh: (the en is nasalized) Seneca "I've seen it."

Agondadonh: (a gawn da dawnh, *ns* are nasalized) Seneca "I'm shaking it."

Charlene Blue Horse

Indian Talk

Three o'clock in the morning
Electrical fire out.
We talk about what's wrong
With Indians, the Reservation.

We are our own worst enemy
Bought the government plan —
Made it ours — Eat white bread
Commods, count blood drops, mail
Frauds, relative deals.

He says; "It's too late, let
The state take over
Indians sleeping with bottles
For warmth and love, our high
Rates, unemployment, alcoholism,
Education. Indians have been
Dying for centuries anyway."

I try to bring hope into blood
And politics while babies
Sleep next door for safety.

The house, cold as yard snow
Five hour wire fire
Broken fire truck, no fighters
Pay won't last to cover sleep.

Can't make jobs from words
Can't restore respect with burnt
Words and wrecked wires
At three o'clock in the morning.

Michael Roberts

Maybe I Should've Worn a Feather

Waiting for the southbound bus to tai chi
class, another night traveler, a short
ugly guy with a mustache and — why me? —
an audible sneer offers a word fart
to me about all these damn got-no-heart
indians dragging their asses around in
marquette's ivy halls. Likely knows my kin.

At the soccer game little jewish
kid's father, wearing a baseball cap, gripes
about those indians spearing all his
muskie. I cough to clear my rusty pipes.
Lucky for him, I look so bad in stripes.
It's grab his throat and get my fingers wet
or stand back mumbling jokes he'll never get.

We go to a vietnamese restaurant
for our anniversary. At the next table
a young upwardly mobile couple can't
stop telling two german tourist dumbbelles,

curious about natives, blind to labels
how the terrible redskins drink their share
and more, sucking up gallons on welfare.

Another time we go to a chinese
eatery with friends and telling how we
sat near these people spouting their malaise,
just then we again break our reverie,
because right beside us more stupidity
those same slurs once more, now more frightening
I go take a leak wary of lightning.

The PTA talks about kid's problem-
solving skills, trying to figure out right
now just how many feet have shoes on them —
I figure I'm in for a real hard night,
when the woman across the table just lights
right up and teehees "Don't count indians —
They got no shoes. They all wear moccasins."

Kimberly Blaeser

Living History

Walked into Pinehurst, sunburned, smelling of fish,
Big Indian man paying for some gas and a six pack,
Looking at me hard.
Dreamer, I think. Too old for me.
Heads right toward me.
"Jeez," he says, "You look just like your mom —
You must be Marlene's girl."
Pinches my arm, but I guess it's yours
he touches.
Hell, wasn't even looking at me.
Wonder if I'm what they call living history?

Charlene Blue Horse

Poem for our Ancestors
Dedicated to the Kiwanis Club

"Look, past the swings and slides
Mounds in a half moon cut off by a street,
Are those mounds ghosts, dancing for peace?"

Almost lost in this big park
A tarnished bronze plaque
Sits in a round rock and reads:

  "Erected 1946
  Marked for education and posterity,
  These circular mounds erected
  by prehistoric mound people."

"Were Mound people short,
Round, ordinary, like this rock?
Were they Candy people
History forgot?"

A cannon guards this park
An American tank, too.
I stand on Sacred circular burial
Grounds marked while Nazis poured Jews
Into trenches.

In 1946, did History know the Holocaust,
Hitler, and forget to write in Indians?
"Sweetheart, our ancestors don't count.
They call them Mound people.

Here, in this Sacred half moon
Ancestors, robbed of peace.
Their broken dance hoop, a circle
Shining through cottonwood. Robbed
By a street, and they marked it.

Indians, Jews, cut in half,
Poured into trenches, mounds.
Marked for education, posterity
And children picnic, play —
Looking for candy bars.

Rose Mary Robinson

When

When winds of change
    Blow strongly through the seasons
And resisting days
    Pass week to week
When with resistance, blowing winds
    Grow stronger,
And the lonely dove, still lonely,
    Flies away —
When mothers leave the nest before their babies,
    And fathers, lean and hungry, looking still —
When children — oh, the children —
    Left to mingle
With the pow'rs beyond belief
    Move into time —
Then we see the world as in a stage-set
    Pretending, as it turns, to be aware
Of the comatose among us slowly dying,
    For lack of caring in a dying world.

Kimberly Blaeser

On the Way to the Chicago Pow-Wow

On the way to the Chicago pow-wow,
Weaving through four-lanes of traffic,
    going into the heart of Carl Sandburg's hog-butcher to
                                      the world,
    ironic, I think, landing at Navy Pier for a pow-wow.
I think of what Roberta said: "Indian people across the
                                    country
    are working on a puzzle, trying to figure out what I call
    —the abyss."
Driving into the abyss. Going to a pow-wow.

On the way to the Chicago pow-wow,
Laugh when I look down at my hands.
Trying to tell you, needing to hear you laugh out loud
    because the puzzle was made by madmen who want us
                                   all lost
    in the rotating maze.
I think my hands have stepped out of Linda Hogan's poem:
One wears silver and turquoise, a Zuni bracelet and a
                                  Navaho ring.

One wears gold and diamonds, an Elgin watch and a
                                        Simonson's half-carat;
The madman's classic mixedblood, a cliche.
Together, laughing out loud at the madness. Going to a
                                        pow-wow.

On the way to the Chicago pow-wow,
Thinking of home, I know we are driving the wrong way.
It's not Lake Michigan I want to see.
It's not Wrigley Field.
But there is no exit here to 113, no cut-across.
I think of Helen's cabin, sitting by the fire drying my hair,
    and Collin talking:
        "Sometimes you have to go in the wrong direction
        to get where you're heading."
Driving southeast, heading northwest. Heading home,
    to White Earth Lake,
    to Indian ball diamonds,
    to open air pow-wow.
Taking the Eden's going to the Chicago pow-wow,
    on the way back home.

Charlene Blue Horse

Feeling Watched

Helicopters, grey government airplanes
Loud rhythmic whirring, droning
Touch close, like a whirlwind or
A monstrous flock of frightened
Geese. An Army of early lawnmowers.

"They scare me." She says. Naomi, dirt
Crusting about her feet and ankles. Goat
Trailing behind, barely visible in tall
Grass. "Why are they over us, when
Will they stop?" Her Hair, eyes, wild.

                    II
I remember back to the Rosebud Reservation.
Watching helicopters, Government airplanes
Dark Grey, circling, circling, three, four
Times a day, close. Frightened pheasants
Scattering, the wild whir of fleeing
Feathers and fear. Horses danced, eyes wild.

III

This is Wisconsin. We just moved here.
Indians run off or massacred long ago,
One woman with children and hair turning
Grey. One Sweat Lodge for prayer,
Purification. A garden, goat, guard
Dog. (They must be learning to fly,
Searching for grey wolves, counting geese.)

IV

Indians on the Reservation, then —
We heard each other's silent wondering
Felt the watching. Our Tribal Chair,
Questioned Government planes. Cottonwoods
Shivered fear. He made them stop watching.

This is Wisconsin, maybe they think one
Woman alone with children, are bringing
Indians back. Maybe they fear the power
Of Indian Women and nine year old girls
Frightened. Must be searching for

Convicts escaped. Still, our fear seeps
Into sleep like a monstrous flock of
Frightened geese, like a whirlwind, lost.

Andrew Connors

Niimi's Song: Traveling Thunder

I'm traveling thunder on tribal wind
The one you seek who lies within
Who can never be put down
I'm changing colors, I move around
In your mind
In your mind I shine

I skirt Creation on twisted ends
Dance with animals and shapeless friends
Like Owl who seems to know
You carry this baggage wherever you go
In your mind
In your mind you are blind

To her sitting by the window
Watching while you go
Running after shadows
And promises in rainbows
Are words that have failed
Now unspoken in the cradle

Lies the eyes of the shadow
Who's running with the rainbow

Se her sitting by a window
Cradling your shadow
He's a two color rainbow
And a word you will never know
Yet you're on another trail.
Wondering why you've failed
But a blowing wind is sailing
Into odysseys and rainbows
Running with us shadows

I toss inside your sheltered mind
A mixed-blood visitor on Indian time
A tribal ghost, a Celtic saint
A crazy picture Creator paints
In your mind we may find

The traveling thunder on tribal winds
Dancing silent while Cedar spins
A Celtic ghost, a tribal dream
And I emerge from within your seams
In our mind
In our mind we will shine

I'm the traveling trickster on tribal winds.

Kenneth Brickman Metoxen

Whitefish Bay
                    Black stone
                                Black lodge
        Ahsiniboine Junior   Eagle Whistle
                    Rocky Boy
                                Sun Eagle
        Beat my heart   Smokey Towne
                    Eagle Plume
                                Elks Voice
        Beat my   Trails
                    heart beat
                                Jingle dress
    Traditional   Fancy Shawl
                With a heart beat
                                Grass
    Fancy   Traditional
                The drum
                        The dance
    The universe   The land
                Life
                    We are
We never were   so therefore

Whitefish Bay . . . Trails: drum groups.

Jingle dress . . . Traditional: categories of pow-wow dancing.

FOR FURTHER INFORMATION:
BOOKS, VIDEOS, NEWSPAPERS

We have tried to present in this very short list a representative selection for people in obtaining further information on Native Americans. Keeping in mind the Wisconsin focus of *Dreaming History*, the following selection has an emphasis on our state. At the same time, we recognize the inadequacy of the items here, keeping in mind the wealth and diversity of Native American civilization. For that reason, we recommend an eighty-page list prepared by Woodland Pattern Book Center of Milwaukee (720 E. Locust; P.O Box 92081, Milwaukee 53202); Schwartz' Bookstore also has an extensive list of Native American information (17145D W. Bluemound Rd, Brookfield, Wis. 53005). Border's Bookstore of Madison carries a good selection of books (3416 University Ave., Madison 53705).

WISCONSIN NATIVE-AMERICANS, GENERAL

Goldstein, Lynn and Robert Ritzenthaler. *Prehistoric Indians of Wisconsin*. Milwaukee Public Museum, 1985.

Hagan, William T. *Sac and Fox Indians*. University of Oklahoma Press, 1958.

Lurie, Nancy Ostreich. *Wisconsin Indians*. State Historical Society of Wisconsin, 1980.

Tanner, Helen Hornbeck. *Atlas of Great Lakes Indian History*. University of Oklahoma, 1987.

Vogel, Virgil J. *Indian Names on Wisconsin's Map*. University of Wisconsin Press, 1991.

ANISHINABE (CHIPPEWA)

Benton-Benai, Eddie. *The Mishomis Book*. Red School House Press, St. Paul, Minn., 1988.

Densmore, Frances. *How the Indians Use Wild Plants for Food, Medicine, Crafts*. Dover Publications, New York, 1974.

Diedrich, Mark, compiler. *Ojibwa Oratory*. Coyote Books, 1991.

Elston, Georgia. *Giving: Ojibwa Stories and Legends*. 1985.

Johnston, Basil. *Ojibwa Ceremonies*. University of Nebraska, 1990.

Johnston, Basil. *Ojibwa Heritage*. University of Nebraska, 1990.

Johnston, Basil. *Ojibwa Tales*. University of Nebraska, 1993.

Northrup, Jim. *Walking the Rez Road*. Voyageur Press, Stillwater, Minn. 1993.

Satz, Ron. *Chippewa Treaty Rights*. Wisconsin Academy of Sciences, Arts and Letters, Madison, 1991.

Slabbert, Loraine, producer & editor. *The Enduring Ways of the Lac du Flambeau People* (video), 1988 (available from Wisconsin Department of Public Instruction; 608-261-6322).

Tanner, Helen Hornbeck. *The Ojibwa*. Chelsea House Publishers, New York, 1992.

Whaley, Rick, with Walt Bresette. *Walleye Warriors*. New Society, 1994.

ANISHINABE (POTAWATAMI)

Edmunds, R. David. *The Potawatamis*. University of Oklahoma Press, 1978.

MENOMINEE

Keesing, Felix M. *The Menominie Indians of Wisconsin*. University of Wisconsin Press, Madison, 1987.

Perhoff, Nicholas C. *Menominee Drums*. University of Oklahoma, 1982.

ONEIDA

Campisi, Jack and Lawrence M. Hauptmann. *The Oneida Indian Experience*. Syracuse University Press, 1988.

MOHICAN (STOCKBRIDGE-MUNSEE)

Frazier, Patrick. *The Mohicans of Stockbridge*. University of Nebraska Press, 1992.

HO'CHUNK (WINNEBAGO)

Diedrich, Mark. *Winnebago Oratory*. Coyote Books, 1991.

Ho'chunk Wo'lduk (newspaper). 133 Main Street, Black River Falls, Wis. 54615.

Mountain Wolf Woman. *Sister of Crashing Thunder; The Autobiography of a Winnebago Woman*, edited by Nancy Ostreich Lurie. University of Michigan Press, 1961.

Riley, Jocelyn, producer. *Her Mother Before Her: Winnebago Women's Stories of Their Mothers & Grandmothers* (video). Her Own Words, 1992 (P.O. Box 5264, Madison, Wis. 53705).

Riley, Jocelyn, producer. *Mountain Wolf Woman* (video). Her Own Words, 1991.

Riley, Jocelyn, producer. *Sisters & Friends* (video). Her Own Words, 1994.

Riley, Jocelyn, producer. *Winnebago Women: Songs & Stories* (video). Her Own Words, 1992.

Tallmadage, Lance and Dave Erickson. *1634: In the Wake of Nicolet* (video). Ootek Productions, 1993.

Tallmadge, Lance and Dave Erickson. *Thunder in the Dells* (video). Ootek Productions, Spring Green, Wis. 1992. (Both available from Little Eagle Trading Co. 1425-2 Wisconsin Dells Parkway, Wisconsin Dells, 53965.)

NATIVE-AMERICANS, GENERAL

Allen, Paula Gunn. *Sacred Hoop: Recovering the Feminine in American Indian Traditions*. Beacon, 1992.

Bruchac, Joseph & Caduto, Michael. *Keepers of the Animals*. Fulcrum, 1991.

Bruchac, Joseph & Caduto, Michael. *Keepers of the Earth*. Fulcrum, 1989.

Bruchac, Joseph & Caduto, Michael. *Keepers of Life*. Fulcrum, 1994.

Bruchac, Joseph. *The Native American Sweat Lodge: History and Legends*. The Crossing Press, 1993.

Champagne, Duane. *Native America: Portrait of the Peoples*. Visible Ink Press, 1994.

Dibadjimo / "They tell stories." Performance of Wisconsin Indian Story Theatre. For information, contact David Peterson, Outreach, Continuing Education–Arts, Room 720, Lowell Hall, University of Wisconsin, Madison, Wis. 53703.

Erdoes, Richard and Alfonso Ortiz, editors. *American Indian Myths & Legends*. Pantheon Books, 1984.

Gill, Sam D. and Irene F. Sullivan. *Dictionary of Native American Mythology*. Oxford University Press, 1992.

Geigomah, Hanay and Michael Grant. *The Native Americans* (video). (Part 1, Northeast; 2, Far West; 3, Southeast; 4, Southwest; 5 & 6, Great Plains). TBS Productions, 1994.

Lyons, Oren, John Mohawk and others. *Exiled in the Land of the Free: Democracy, Indian Nations, and the U.S. Constitution*. Clear Light Publishers, 1992.

News From Indian Country (newspaper). Rt. 2, Box 2900-A, Hayward, Wis. 54843.

Sams, Jamie & David Carson. *Medicine Cards: The Discovery of Power Through the Ways of Animals*. Bear & Company, 1988.

Sams, Jamie. *Sacred Path Cards: The Discovery of Self Through Native Teachings*. Harper San Francisco, 1990.

Schneider, Richard C. *Crafts of the North American Indians*. R. Schneider Publishers, Stevens Point, Wis. 1972.

Wall, Steve and Harvey Arden. *Wisdom Keepers: Meetings with Native American Spiritual Leaders*. Beyond Words, 1990.

Wall, Steve. *Wisdom's Daughters: Conversations with Women Elders of Native North America*. HarperCollins, 1993.

Weatherford, Jack. *Indian Givers*. Fawcett, 1990.

Weatherford, Jack. *Native Roots: How the Indians Enriched the Americas*. Fawcett, 1992.

Kimberly M. Blaeser, of Ojibwa and German ancestry from White Earth reservation in Minnesota, is currently an Assistant Professor of English and Comparative Literature at University of Wisconsin-Milwaukee. Her study of Gerald Vizenor will appear from University of Oklahoma Press, and a collection of poetry, *Trailing You*, from Greenfield Review Press.

Charlene Blue Horse, Oglala Lakota, has taught Creative Writing and Literature since 1972 at schools such as Sinte Gleska College and more recently University of Wisconsin-La Crosse. She currently lives on a forty-acre farm near Stoddard, Wisconsin.

Andrew Connors, Bad River Ojibwe, is editor of *Migizi Express*, the newsletter of Milwaukee Indian Community newsletter. He studied at University of Wisconsin-Milwaukee, where he received a Master's degree. He is of Ojibwa ancestry.

Ellen Kort, of Ojibwa ancestry, received the Pablo Neruda Literary Award in 1992. Her play *Glory of the Morning* was performed during the 1992 Paper Arts Festival in Apppleton. Her work will be performed in conjunction with the Martha Graham Company of New York City in 1995.

Pamela Green LaBarge works for the Oneida Career Development and Technical Training Center, and is the first chair of Oneida Nation Arts Program. She recently received a Masters Degree in Creative Writing from University of Wisconsin-Milwaukee.

Kenneth Brickman Metoxen, member of Oneida Nation of Wisconsin, has worked there as Director of Oneida Museum and more recently as Community Arts Director. He has a Master's degree in Art from University of Wisconsin-Madison.

Gladyce Nahbenayash is a Bear Clan member of the Original Band of Lake Superior Chippewa. She is an Assistant Professor of American Indian Studies and counselor at University of Wisconsin-Superior.

Michael Roberts, a member of the Turtle Clan of Oneida Nation, works as librarian at Milwaukee Indian Community School. He has a Master's degree in English with Creative Writing concentration from University of Wisconsin-Milwaukee.

Rose Mary Robinson, of Ojibwa ancestry, was a vice-president of Honor, Inc. She recently received a Master's degree in Counseling Psychology from University of Wisconsin-Milwaukee. She is presently residing in Northern Wisconsin.

Mary Anne Doan has been Native American Outreach Specialist for CESA 5 in Portage. She currently resides in Albuquerque, New Mexico and is of Cree ancestry.

Jim Stevens' recent works have included *The Journey Home* (North Country Press) and *An August Derleth Reader* (Prairie Oak Press). He has taught at University of Wisconsin-La Crosse, University of Wisconsin-Madison Arts Outreach, and worked as Editor at Stanton & Lee Publishers. He is of Seneca and German ancestry.